Craft Cider Making

THIRD EDITION

Andrew Lea

THE CROWOOD PRESS

First published in 2008 by the GoodLife Press

This edition published in 2015 by
The Crowood Press Ltd
Ramsbury, Marlborough
Wiltshire SN8 2HR

enquiries@crowood.com

www.crowood.com

This impression 2023

British Library Cataloguing-in-Publication Data
A catalogue record for this book is available from the British Library.

ISBN 978 1 78500 015 7

Acknowledgements
Too many people in the UK and overseas have contributed to my thinking for this book for
me to acknowledge them all individually. The rise of the internet has created a worldwide
craft cider community from which I am always learning. But I would especially like to
thank Liz Copas for her comments on orcharding, Dick Dunn for many helpful discussions
of small scale cidermaking in general, Rose Grant and Mark Powell for permission
to photograph their cider houses, and Ray Blockley for supplying some of his own
photographs. As for the rest of you, you know who you are!

Typeset by Servis Filmsetting Ltd, Stockport, Cheshire
Printed and bound in India by Parksons Graphics

CONTENTS

PREFACE

Just over fifty years ago a little book called *Cider Making* was published in the Countryman's Library (Hart Davis, 1957). It was written for the amateur by Alfred Pollard and Fred Beech, two scientists at the Long Ashton Horticultural Research Station, which had been founded in 1903 in a small village just outside Bristol. By the 1950s Long Ashton was the premier Cider Research Station in the world and had become a major centre of horticultural research. Now the site where it once stood is a housing estate.

I was privileged to work at the Research Station in its later years, from 1972 until 1985, when the Cider Section closed. Much of what is in this book I learnt from my time at Long Ashton and from colleagues such as Fred Beech, Len Burroughs, Geoff Carr, Colin Timberlake, Ray Williams, and many, many more. Now that the Long Ashton Research Station is gone for good, I would like to dedicate this little book to its memory and to the memory of the men and women who worked there and who taught me so much. I hope this book will be a worthy and useful successor to the original *Cider Making* of half a century ago.

I would further like to dedicate it to my family who have indulged and helped me in my hobby for so long and, in particular, to my dear wife Josephine who was my Chief Assistant Cider Maker for so many years.

Andrew Lea

INTRODUCTION

This book is aimed at anyone who wants to learn how to grow cider apples and to make good cider. You might have inherited a back garden with a couple of apple trees or several acres of derelict orchard in an idyllic rural setting. You might be 'scrumping' apples from friends and neighbours every autumn or buying juice from someone who has a press. You might be planting a tiny suburban plot or you might be planting up an entire field. Either way, you want to learn how to make cider and this book is designed for all of you. It is aimed primarily at a UK readership but I hope will be of value to other English-speaking cider makers in North America, Australasia and elsewhere, and I have tried not to forget them.

The cider you make from this book will not be like most of what you can buy on the supermarket shelf or in a town centre bar. This book will not tell you how to make a Magners or a Strongbow 'clone'. It will not tell you how to make an alcopop style cider flavoured with herbs or other fruits, and it will not give you any 'recipes', because craft cider making is never just a matter of mixing ingredients together for a predictable result. Rather, this book aims to give you sufficient technique to be able to make cider in a way that retains the best of traditional practice, while drawing on the best modern understanding of orcharding and fermentation science. It is primarily for people working on a small scale, which could be as little as 10 litres every year up to say 10,000 litres. Larger than that and you will be verging on the industrial scale. That is not to say you cannot make good cider on a large scale – you can, but with scale come additional layers

of logistical and business considerations which are not dealt with in this book. However, the fundamental principles of cider making remain the same irrespective of scale.

There has never been a time quite like the present for an interest in cider in the English-speaking world. Although this is due in part to zealous marketing by the mainstream commercial operations, it is also a reflection of an increasing interest in 'slow-food' and the connection between our food and the land on which it grows. In the temperate zones of the world the production chain between growing the fruit, making the cider and enjoying the product can be as short as a few yards. 'Food miles' for cider can be minimal.

In this introduction we look first at the history of cider and its international distribution, and look at the definition and basic production of cider. In Chapter 1 we take an overview of the cider making process from the fruit onwards, and in later chapters we go into each aspect more fully. Finally, there are chapters on trouble shooting and on making unfermented apple juice and cider vinegar. At the end of the book there is a list of other sources of information (since no single book has all the answers!) and suppliers of both trees and equipment.

HISTORICAL BACKGROUND

Cider has been known in Britain for around a thousand years. It seems to have been made

Title pages from the third (1691) edition of *Vinetum Britannicum*.

in the Mediterranean basin around the time of Pliny (first century AD), and it became well-established in Normandy and Brittany in early medieval times (from 800 AD onwards), probably moving northwards from the Atlantic coast of Spain where cider is still made. It is not clear whether cider was made in Britain in the Anglo-Saxon period, but after the Norman Conquest it certainly seems to have taken hold here, and the first mention of established production in this country is from Norfolk in 1205. During the seventeenth and eighteenth centuries, in the stability following the English Civil War, it seemed to have reached something of a zenith with cider being compared to the best French wines and exported from the West Country to London. A

number of manuals on the subject were published at this time, including John Worlidge's famous *Vinetum Britannicum – A Treatise on Cider and Perry*, which was first published in 1678. John Evelyn, the diarist, politician and arboriculturalist, published his *Pomona* in 1664, which discusses fruit growing in general and cider making in particular, and included contributions from authors throughout the country. *Pomona* (part of his epic *Sylva*) went through several editions in the following century.

Educated and landed gentlemen such as Isaac Newton, on his family estate in Lincolnshire, are known to have been cider makers. Knowledge of its manufacture was exported to the new North American colonies (Connecticut cider is mentioned by Evelyn) and later it became a favoured drink of Thomas Jefferson, third President of the United States, who grew cider apples on his estate at Monticello, Virginia. In 1797 Thomas Andrew Knight from Herefordshire (a founder of the Royal Horticultural Society) first published his *Treatise on the Culture of the Apple and Pear, and the Manufacture of Cider and Perry*, which passed through four later editions. William Coxe from New Jersey, US, one of Knight's correspondents, published his *View of the Cultivation of Fruit Trees, and the Management of Orchards and Cider*, the first American fruit book, in 1817. In other countries cider making was also of interest – indeed the very first known cider making manual had been published in France by Julien le Paulmier in 1589 – and throughout the nineteenth century books on the topic appeared in France, Germany and Spain.

For many years cider was made over all the southern and midland counties of England, even into Yorkshire, although the centre of UK cider production eventually became consolidated in a band stretching northwards from Devon and Cornwall through Somerset, Dorset, Gloucestershire, Worcestershire and Herefordshire, with sporadic local operations in the East Midlands, East Anglia, Kent, Hampshire and Sussex. Cider rather than beer became the typical alcoholic drink of the west of England, perhaps in part because the climate there was too wet for growing malting barley successfully. Certainly by the time of Evelyn and Worlidge, who were both making cider themselves in the south-east of England, there was already an appreciation of the fact that the best ciders came from the counties which lay further to the west.

In the UK cider did not seem to withstand the challenge of imported wines nor the ascendancy of beer, and by the end of the nineteenth century it seems to have been made without much care and attention on most West Country farms. It was often considered as 'truck' or a part of the labourers' wages, particularly at harvest time when last season's cider would be consumed, a practice finally abolished by the Truck Act of 1887.

It was the associated decline in quality, much lamented by the Bath and West Show Committee in Somerset during the 1890s, which led to the eventual formation of the National Fruit and Cider Institute at Long Ashton near Bristol in 1903, to improve the quality and technical understanding of cider manufacture. Influential landowners in cider areas, such as Robert Neville Grenville of Butleigh in Somerset and Charles Radcliffe Cooke who was MP for Hereford, were prime movers in the new scientific approach to cider making. Together with the growth of rail transport and bottling technology this understanding soon enabled a new cider market to be established in towns and cities throughout the twentieth century, eventually dominated by a few large manufacturers. Now, in the first part of the twenty-first century, there is a new divergence between the mass-market producers on the one hand and the smaller specialist 'craft' producers on the other.

In the United States, as in the UK, cider was supplanted by beer during the nineteenth century and was eventually almost extinguished by the Temperance and Prohibition movements. The very word 'cider' in the US had its meaning changed by the prohibitionists to indicate a fresh apple juice rather than the fermented product. Now, however, a new craft cider revival has begun in the United States and Canada, and in Australia and New Zealand too.

THE MODERN PRODUCT

Most UK cider is made by just a few large manufacturers. At the time of writing the two largest and most widely known names are Bulmers, once a Herefordshire family company now owned by the brewer Heineken, and Gaymers (once Taunton Cider and Showerings) now owned by the Irish C&C Group. Magners (aka Bulmers Ireland) is also a part of C&C. Another major producer of 'own-label' ciders, although largely unknown to the general public, is Aston Manor, a Birmingham brewer. Westons, Thatchers, Sheppys and Aspall are all family-owned cider makers with national supermarket distribution. Behind them on the supermarket shelf come other independent brands such as Dunkertons, Henneys and Burrow Hill.

Finally, there are now hundreds of smaller craft producers – it is believed there may be as many as 350 of these. Their products will never have a national listing, but often they are locally available through farmers' markets, agricultural shows, village shops and pubs. All this serves to indicate that the diversity of ciders now available in the UK is both healthy and varied. In other countries the production and distribution patterns are of course different, but in North America and Australasia there has been a similar trend, and both the 'industrial' and 'craft' cider markets have seen considerable growth and increased customer interest in recent years.

WHAT IS CIDER AND HOW IS IT PRODUCED?

In the UK cider is understood and defined by Her Majesty's Revenue and Customs (HMRC) to be a beverage made 'wholly or partly from the fermented juice of apples'. Similar words (*cidre, sidra*) are also used in France and Spain. In Germany, Austria and Switzerland, where much small scale cider is made, there is no specific word and the term *Apfelwein* is generally used in addition to local dialect terms such as *Ebbelwoi, Stoffsche, Viez* and *Most*. In the US and Canada the word 'cider' commonly refers to a cloudy but unfermented 'farmgate' apple juice unless qualified by the term 'hard cider' to denote that it has been fermented, and this can be a source of some confusion.

Springtime in the orchard.

According to the Oxford English Dictionary the word 'cider' itself is derived from Greek or even Hebrew sources and simply means 'strong drink', although a millennium of usage now ties it in with apples. Although many British people imagine that cider is uniquely British, with some possible concession to the French, this is really not the case. Cider of some sort has historically been made almost everywhere that apples are grown, with the probable exception of south and south-east Asia. Nevertheless, the greatest bulk of commercial cider is currently made in the UK (at around 900 million litres annually), followed by France, Spain, Ireland, Germany and Switzerland. South Africa is also a large producer in volume terms but their definition of cider allows a wider fruit wine base and flavour addition than in most other countries.

It might be reasonable for people to assume that cider is made entirely from apples. In many countries this is laid down by law, but in the UK the minimum legal juice content in cider is 35 per cent and other fermenting sugars are also permitted. Hence the UK market leading brands are made mostly from glucose syrup (*circa* 50–65 per cent) with smaller amounts of apple (*circa* 50–35 per cent), a fortification practice which is known (erroneously) as 'chaptalization'. These are fermented to high alcohol and then diluted with water before sale. This lighter style of 'cider' has achieved great popularity since the 1970s but bears little relationship to the product made entirely from apples – in the craft cider community these are known disparagingly as 'glucose wines'.

Although most of the apples that are used in these ciders are UK sourced, consuming about 50 per cent of all apples grown in the UK, a significant amount of the apple solids content is derived from apple juice concentrate, which is an intermediate raw material prepared by vacuum removal of water to give a high solids syrup which can be stored for months or years

At work in a small cider shed.

without the risk of fermenting. This saves on tank volume and also enables cider to be made all year round rather than seasonally. Much of this concentrate is prepared 'in house' from dedicated cider apple fruit, augmented by dessert concentrate bought on the world market, in which China is now the largest supplier. All this makes commercial sense, but arguably the best quality ciders are those made from domestic single strength apple juice as the primary raw material. That is the 'craft' cider making which this book is about.

Made like wine, not like beer

It is important to understand that cider is a fruit wine. It is not a beer. Anyone with experience of brewing should try to forget most of it when starting to make cider! To be a cider maker you need to think like a winemaker from the beginning. Craft cider, like wine, is a seasonal product. It is made in the autumn, ferments and matures in the winter and spring, and is ready to drink from the summer of the following year. Mainstream commercial ciders are made from stored ingredients on a two-week cycle throughout the year, but craft cider is not like that. Beer, likewise, can be made from stored barley, glucose syrup and dried hops or extract whenever the brewer wishes. Not so for craft cider.

There are many myths around traditional craft cider which have been mistakenly and incorrectly borrowed from traditional brewing – for instance, the idea that cider is best served cloudy from a cask and must contain 'live' yeast. Nobody would expect this for wine, and nobody should expect it for cider either. Likewise, there is a pervasive 'muck and magic' myth that to make traditional craft cider all that is necessary is to run apple juice into a wooden cask and let it ferment 'naturally' without any other attention! This may, by good luck, produce a superb cider but all too often it is acetic, murky, full of strange odours and really quite unpleasant to drink, except to the committed fanatic or to the unsuspecting tourist who expects no better of his 'scrumpy'. If this is the sort of cider you want to make and drink, then do not read this book!

Cider and the law

In the UK there is no restriction on cider making for home consumption by family and friends. If you intend to sell any of it then you must be registered with Her Majesty's Revenue and Customs (HMRC), to comply with Customs and Excise

Notice 162, which lays down permitted ingredients and practices and the 'duty' regulations. Until 2015 a small producer could make up to 7,000 litres of cider for sale without paying duty. However, this exemption is in breach of EU directives, and at the time of writing the future duty status for small producers is uncertain.

To sell the cider direct to the public (as distinct from wholesale), other licensing issues (such as 'premises' and 'personal' licences) come into play, for which advice must be obtained from your local District Council as the licensing authority. Bottled cider must also fulfil appropriate criteria laid down in food content and labelling law, as advised by Trading Standards.

Finally but very importantly, under the Food Safety Act, anyone producing cider for sale must register as a 'Food Producer' with their local District Council Environmental Health Department. They will wish to inspect your premises, and as for any food manufacturing operation you should have a HACCP plan (Hazard Analysis of Critical Control Points) drawn up for what you do. Cider for sale in the UK should comply with the National Association of Cider Makers (NACM) Code of Practice, which is for the most part identical to C&E Notice 162.

The law in other countries differs widely from that in the UK and will not be covered here.

An Englishman's Home

The phrase 'an Englishman's home is his castle' was coined in 1763 by William Pitt during a parliamentary debate on the taxation of cider which allowed Excise men to enter private homes to see if cider was being produced there.

1 WHAT DO I NEED TO MAKE CIDER?

The minimum basic requirements for cider making are apples, some form of crusher or mill to prepare the pulp, a press to yield the juice, and vessels of various sorts in which to ferment and store the cider. (See below for a more comprehensive list, most items being described in more detail throughout the book.)

MATERIALS

Because of its acidity, only certain types of materials should be allowed to come into contact with apple juice and cider.

What Will I Need?

Equipment

Boxes, buckets, poles and 'pankers' (for harvesting and fruit storage);

Apple washing and sorting equipment;

Mill (crusher) and press;

Pulp containers;

Food-grade buckets and pails (for juice collection);

Fermentation tanks and airlocks;

Food-grade electric pump and hoses (optional);

Storage vessels, bottles, kegs, flexible bags, seals and caps;

Pasteurizer (optional).

Sundries and consumables (as required)

Hydrometer to monitor the progress of fermentation;

pH strips or pH meter;

Acidity titration kit;

Yeast;

Campden tablets or metabisulphite powder;

Brushes and cleansing/sterilizing agents;

Syphon and racking tubes and hoses;

Food grade scoops, buckets, jugs, funnels and strainers;

Clean wooden broom handle for stirring pulp and clearing blockages;

Strong rubber gloves with roughened palms;

Waterproof apron;

Turkey baster for sampling.

Infrastructure

Clean water supply and hose;

Sheltered and well-lit working area with drainage.

Metals

Most metals should be avoided, with the notable exception of food-grade stainless steel, which is excellent but costly. Of the two common grades, 316 SS is preferred, since 304 SS is more prone to corrosion by the malic acid of cider over time. Brass, bronze and aluminium are permissible for short contact periods only. Iron, mild steel and copper should never be in contact with cider or juice because they dissolve in the fruit acid to give strange flavours and colours from black to green, although traditional scratter mills with cast iron teeth may be used providing they are well rinsed with clean water after each session of use to restrict corrosion.

Lead is particularly dangerous because it dissolves to give a sweet compound which is potentially fatal. Indeed, in the eighteenth century when the so-called 'Devonshire colic' claimed a number of lives this was eventually discovered to be due to lead poisoning caused by cider which became contaminated when standing in lead pipes overnight in pubs and inns. Similarly, the old practice of lining juice tubs or press trays with lead sheeting to prevent leakage is highly dangerous.

Wood

Wood, of course, was for many years the only practicable material for fermentation and storage vats, and the cooper's art was a skilled and important one. Nowadays wood is regarded as more difficult to manage and harder to keep clean and free from spoilage organisms than the more modern synthetic alternatives. Wood coated with modern polyurethane varnish (for press racks, for example) is much easier to keep clean than unsealed wood.

For fermentation and storage tanks, food-grade stainless steel, plastics, fibreglass and epoxy resins are generally preferable to wood because they contain no pores where undesirable bacteria and moulds can lurk. Glass is also very satisfactory on a small scale for hobby use or for trial batches.

CLEANING/SANITIZING

It should go without saying that as a general rule all equipment and containers in contact with juice or cider should be well cleaned (and well rinsed if necessary) beforehand.

Modern sterilizing detergents which have been designed for food equipment use (such as VWP) are intended both to clean and to sanitize, and are most effective in this role. They are typically based on active oxygen (for example, peracetic acid or peroxycarbonates) or active

Typical chlorine-based sanitizer and cleaner.

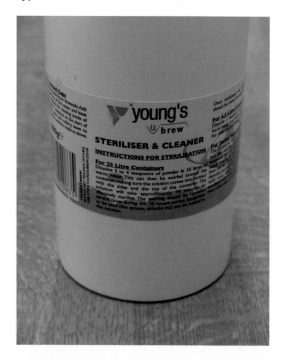

chlorine (such as dichloroisocyanurate) to act as sanitizers, and are also formulated with a low-foaming surfactant (detergent) so they are easy to rinse away. There are also some no-rinse preparations on the market some of which (like Star San) are based on phosphoric acid as a sanitizer. Such sanitizer/cleaners are available from home-brew shops and should be used according to the manufacturer's directions. Do not use regular household detergents or bleach, since they are often perfumed and the suds can be difficult to rinse away fully.

When buying any container for cider making, it is worth asking yourself the question 'how can I get inside to clean and sterilize this?' Small narrow-necked containers such as demi-johns or larger containers with small hatches such as IBCs (Intermediate Bulk Containers) can prove particularly problematic, though specialist ball-head spray nozzles can be bought for IBCs.

If you particularly want to use wooden barrels, make sure that they are well scoured and rinsed or steamed beforehand, and that they do not smell in any way musty. They can be cleaned with 'washing soda' solution (75g of sodium carbonate dissolved in 5 litres of boiling water) filled into the barrel and rolled around at intervals for half an hour. After rinsing well with clean water, they should also be 'sweetened' and stored wet with a sulphur dioxide solution made from 10g of sodium metabisulphite and 10g of citric acid dissolved in 5 litres of water. This solution should be changed every three months and washed out before the barrel is used. It is not advisable to use any form of bleach or chlorine-based cleaner on wooden barrels, because this can set up chemical reactions (formation of chlorophenols) which may later taint the cider. Barrel staves should not be allowed to dry out or they may leak.

A small neat cider house showing a hydraulic pack press on the right and variable capacity stainless steel tanks in the background.

Cider house showing a 'trumpet' mill on the left, with sink and bottle drainer to the rear.

THE FRUIT

Dessert *vs* juice apples

Cider can be made from almost any type of apple. In the Eastern Counties of England (Suffolk, Kent and Sussex), surplus dessert apples such as Cox, Jonagold and Russets are used to produce a light and relatively acidic style of cider.

A similar style of cider is made in Germany and Switzerland from dessert apples and from traditional named cider apples such as Bohnapfel, Borsdorfer and Blauacher. These apples however tend to be more acidic and much lower in tannin than would be regarded as ideal for cider in the West Country or France. Little distinction is made between cider and juice apples and the ciders are very acceptable locally, although somewhat thin and acidic to an English palate. In Spain the traditional cider apples are sharp but slightly tannic.

In northeastern US or Canada, with a long history of cider making from colonial times, typical varieties might be Golden Russet, Roxbury Russet, Northern Spy and Cortland, although many keen amateurs are now planting English 'bittersweets'. UK apples do not necessarily do well in North America due to lack of winter chilling in the warmer climates and too much winter cold elsewhere. Fireblight susceptibility can also be a problem. However, non-traditional cider areas such as the Pacific Northwest coast, with cool damp climates similar to the UK or Normandy, do seem to be more suitable for the European varieties.

In Australia and New Zealand, ciders are typically made from dessert apples often taken from cold store, but an increasing number of growers are also planting or top-working British and French cider varieties. Lack of winter chilling in the warmer parts of southern Australia can reduce the yields of these 'true' cider apples.

The true cider apple

It must be admitted that much of the mystique of cider making does lie with the selection of 'true' cider apples – that is, those cultivars raised and grown for no other purpose and indeed often regarded as inedible.

In the West Country and in northwest France, where arguably the finest ciders are made, these are centred on the high-tannin 'Bittersweet' and 'Bittersharp' varieties (if low in tannin, these are correspondingly described as 'Sweets' or 'Sharps'). Since these are generally unavailable on the open market except in glut years, anyone planting a new cider orchard in the UK would be well-advised to select and grow these 'true' cider apples. Not only do they have the extra 'body' and 'bite' due to high tannin, but they also press much more easily than dessert apples due to their fibrous structure. Some of these varieties, at least, also possess the elusive character of 'vintage quality' which sets apart the best cider from the run of the mill. But if you do not have these apples, do not despair – you can make a very drinkable cider, even though it may not possess the depth and richness of the best West Country or Norman examples.

Tannin and acidity

A word about 'tannin' is probably in order here, since it is so frequently mentioned in connection with cider and yet is so frequently confused with acidity. This is perhaps because both acidity and tannin are high in most 'crab' apples (which are hardly ever the true species, merely domestic apples which have gone wild from seed).

Acidity is easy to understand – a lemon provides a good example of this. Tannin is exemplified by the mouth-puckering taste of strong tea, or by the taste of a sloe berry – it can be both bitter and/or astringent ('hard' or 'soft'), depending on its chemical structure and molecular size. Chemically, tannin in cider is a synonym for certain types of complex flavonoid polyphenols (the procyanidins), which are also responsible for the browning of apples as they oxidize.

In cider making we need both tannin and acidity in moderate amounts, as will be explained later. The other major component we need from the apple is sugar to ferment into alcohol. 'True' cider apples tend to give higher sugar levels than regular dessert apples, which is another reason for choosing them. They are also typically easier to press.

MILLING AND PRESSING

Apples are hard fruits and so, whatever kinds of apples are used, they must first be milled to a pulp before the juice can be pressed out. These are two distinct operations, which is rather different from winemaking where the grapes need only a light crushing to break the skins before expressing the juice.

Broxwood Foxwhelp cider fruit.

Milling

Traditionally apple milling was done in a circular stone trough by a rotating stone wheel drawn round by a horse. From the eighteenth century onwards stone or wooden roller mills based on two closely spaced but contra-rotating shafts were used, powered either by hand or steam.

'Scratter', or grater mills, in which a wheel bearing coarse knives or graters rotates against a fixed surface, are also popular and form the basis of the high-speed mills used in most modern cider factories. Domestic versions of this mill are also available. Centrifugal hammer or knife mills are somewhat cheaper. At worst, a food processor or a thick lump of timber may be used to smash the fruit to a pulp, or a rotating blade ('Pulpmaster') may be harnessed to the end of an electric drill. Resourceful people have modified in-line waste disposal units, or even garden shredders, but care must be taken regarding safety issues, protection of the motor from wet pulp and ensuring construction from suitable acid-proof materials. A variety of mills

Inside a 'trumpet' mill. Two rotating knife blades and two pushers are arranged in a cross and the removable screen controls the pulp size.

An 'edge runner' horse-powered mill at the Hereford Cider Museum. In use, apples would have been piled in the centre and pushed into the trough for grinding by the stone wheel.

Feeding a Speidel fruit mill.

Feeding a Voran scratter mill.

The rotating knife assembly inside a Speidel mill with its vertical and horizontal blades.

The wooden blocks push the fruit towards the rotating knife drum, and the milled fruit drops through the small gap to its left.

at various prices is now available from specialist suppliers or there are plans available on the web (*see* Resources).

Pressing

To extract the juice from the pulp, wooden screw 'pack' presses were used from medieval times onwards. The apple pulp had first to be built into a 'cheese' using alternate thin layers of pulp and straw. Pressure was then applied to the cheese, usually by a large wooden screw, the straw providing drainage channels so that juice could flow to a receiving tray and thence to a barrel as the compressed pulp diminished in volume. This principle is still used in many modern cider presses, both large and small. The straw has long since been replaced by wooden

A traditional straw press on a wooden base.

or plastic slats and woven synthetic cloths, and the pressure is now provided by an hydraulic pump, but the principle of making the cheese still remains.

Small-scale presses

Small-scale pack presses are readily available from specialist suppliers, or they can be made at home (several plans are available on the web; *see* Resources). In the homemade version a bottle jack in a hardwood frame or a commercial steel-framed screw press bed forms the motive power. Juice yields of 70 per cent or upwards are possible with good design.

Small-scale basket presses are relatively cheap and widely available for domestic use, being commonly used for grapes, but they may give rather poor juice yields on apples (about 50 per cent) because no proper allowance is made for

A traditional double screw press and stone base in Herefordshire. Note the lack of racks between the cloths.

A home-built pack press using a bottle jack.

A simple hand-turned knife mill on top of a basket press.

Basket press and chopped apples. Note that such coarse pulp gives a very low juice yield.

drainage channels in the pulp and not all the juice can find an easy pathway out.

Hydraulic 'bladder press'

A new development for the small scale cider maker, although used for many years in commercial wineries, is the hydraulic 'bladder press'. The pulp is placed in a perforated stainless steel drum, together with a rubber 'bladder'. No electric power is required; the bladder is inflated by mains water pressure and squeezes the juice out through the perforated drum. Juice yields for apples of around 60 per cent are generally claimed, but the mill needs to be custom designed to give a finely divided pulp which really suits the press; hence the mill and press are typically sold as a pair. For hobby use, such a press is much cheaper and easier to clean and maintain than a powered hydraulic press and

Filling the Speidel cage, with mesh cloth in place.

Speidel press showing the deflated bladder in the steel cage.

Speidel press working, with splash screen in place.

hence may be a cost effective solution for the amateur.

Automated press

There is no 'scaled-down' version of the most popular semi-continuous commercial press, the automated Bucher-Guyer horizontal piston press which is used in most of the larger cider factories; it comprises flexible nylon drainage channels running throughout an enclosed steel cylinder which is filled with pulp 'on demand' and gradually compressed. Such presses can handle several tons of apples per hour, night and day, yet are operated by just one person sitting at a control panel.

An intermediate and cheaper form of operation is offered by the Bucher Multi Press which combines the technology of flexible drainage channels with the mechanical simplicity of the bladder press.

Belt presses, where a thin layer of pulp is squeezed continuously between two endless woven steel and nylon belts, were originally developed for sewage sludge de-watering, but have recently become popular in commercial juice and cider factories, although they tend to lack some flexibility in adjusting to variable fruit quality. Smaller versions of these do exist and are sold into the craft cider making community, but due to their cost and high throughput are not likely to be of interest to most readers of this book.

Juice extractors

At completely the other end of the scale it is possible to make a few litres of juice using a kitchen juice extractor. The type that comprises a metal grater plate and a basket centrifuge to separate the juice from the pulp can work well, but is generally designed to handle only a few fruits at a time and can rapidly suffer from excessive pulp build-up.

However, there are larger semi-commercial versions now available for juice bar use, and some people have found they can be adapted to produce juice in sufficient quantities for small scale cider making. A feature of the method, which is known by its advocates as 'Juice and Strain', is that as soon as it is produced the juice is strained through fine net to remove excess pulp material. Two juicers are required so that one can be cooling off while the other is in use, because they are not designed for continuous usage and the motors can overheat and burn out if run for too long.

Freezer

Also on a small scale it is possible to freeze fruits in a deep freeze for a couple of days or longer and then allow them to thaw. Only a light squeeze is then needed to extract the juice from the disrupted pulp, thus obviating the need for either a mill or a serious press. Some people report good results by this method.

Outlay

The greatest unavoidable capital cost for a craft cider maker is probably always incurred in acquiring the mill and press, even if home-made, and for any scale of operation in excess of 10 or 20 litres an investment of several hundred pounds may be anticipated if commercial equipment is being purchased. Unlike containers and other ancillaries, the milling and pressing equipment is often more difficult to scrounge and adapt. On the other hand, good equipment should last for many years if well maintained and always has some resale value. Indeed, second-hand equipment, carefully vetted, is a good route for the beginner. But do your research before parting with your money.

FERMENTATION AND STORAGE

A good yield of juice from apples is typically around 75 per cent, so from 100kg of apples around 75 litres of juice and cider may be obtained. Once that juice is expressed, sufficient fermentation and storage capacity is essential. This can range from 5 litre glass demi-johns up to 1000 litre 'IBC' plastic tanks or even stainless steel tanks (note that in North America the term 'demi-john' typically refers to a glass vessel around 50 litres in size). All containers should be 'food grade', easy to clean and capable of being kept tightly closed (both with and without a fermentation lock).

Second-hand plastic

With care it is possible to re-use containers which have contained other foodstuffs and are cheaply available second hand, for instance the grey plastic ex-fruit juice concentrate drums. Check before you buy, though, since some of these are so badly tainted that they cannot be used for cider making. The plastic can adsorb high impact flavour compounds which gradually leach out into the new liquid over many

Re-used tanks that previously held fruit juice concentrate.

filling and emptying cycles (a process known as 'flavour scalping'). This happens no matter how frequently you clean or steam the containers.

In general, plastic tanks that have previously contained citrus or blackcurrant juice or oils, or any form of spice extract, are unsuitable for use with cider. However, drums that have previously contained apple juice, grape juice or even olives and vegetable oils generally prove to be quite satisfactory. The flavour compounds released from these materials do not have adverse characteristics which would taint the cider.

A collection of tanks including two IBCs in the centre.

Tanks

Purpose-designed HDPE (high-density polyethylene) tanks sold for small-scale winemaking are ideal for cider fermentation and may be obtained in sizes from around 50–500 litres. A cheaper solution is provided by the widely available 220 litre blue food grade barrels which are humorously known in cider circles as 'blue oak', although these can be more difficult to keep airtight and they are not generally supplied with airlocks or taps, which the user needs to fit.

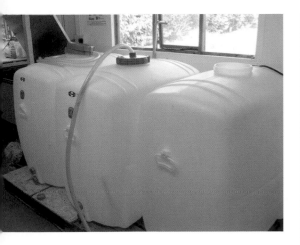

Purpose-designed HDPE fermentation tanks.

Both types of tank have wide necks which makes cleaning easy, whereas the standard IBC shape does not (though it is possible to buy specialist spray cleaning heads for them).

It is worth remembering that any full tank will probably be immoveable since the carrying

'Blue Oak' food-grade drums used for fermentation. (Photo: Ray Blockley)

A handy cider house pump.

handles, if provided, are for use only when the tank is empty. So tanks must be filled where they are to remain (or placed on pallets so they can be moved by pallet truck). For this reason a small electric pump is a valuable accessory for the cider maker.

Racking

During yeast fermentation the juice sugars turn to alcohol and other important flavour changes take place. Once complete, the cider is 'racked' by pumping or siphoning away from the yeast into a clean container for further storage, so that at least one extra empty container is required to act as a 'holding tank' during racking. After racking and maybe blending, a further period of maturation may be required.

The Final Product

One of the most difficult decisions, but one which the cider maker may need to contemplate even before the cider is made, is the type of final product and its packaging. Is it to be dry, sweet, still, carbonated, in a bottle, in a cask or in a bag-in-box? These questions are not trivial since some of these are much more difficult for the craft cider maker to achieve than others, and some are mutually incompatible. As consumers we are so familiar with the sweetened, carbonated version of cider available on the supermarket shelves that we may not realize quite how much technology it entails compared to the production of a simple still dry cider.

To make good craft cider the right sort of yeast must be present and it must dominate other less desirable organisms. There must be sufficient nutrient in addition to sugar for the yeast to grow. It must convert much of the sugar to alcohol and it must also generate desirable flavour characteristics as it does so. After fermentation most or all of the yeast should be removed and the cider stored in the absence of air, protected from spoilage yeasts and bacteria until opened for consumption. Exactly how we achieve these objectives is the subject of the following chapters.

To conclude here is an outline process chart showing the unit operations involved in cider making, with options which any individual cider maker may choose to exercise as he or she wishes. These options are discussed in detail throughout the book.

Cider Making Process Chart

Main Process	Options
Apple sourcing	Varietal selection Nutrient levels
Harvesting	
Storage	Fruit blending
Washing	
Milling	Storage of pulp Pectinase addition
Pressing and juice preparation	Keeving, pectinase addition pH (acidity) adjustment SO_2 addition, yeast addition Nutrient addition
Fermentation	Addition of sugar (chaptalization)
Racking	Malo-lactic fermentation SO_2 addition Natural (arrested) sweetening
Storage in bottle or cask	Blending, fining, filtration Added sweetener and preservative SO_2 addition Carbonation Pasteurization

2 CIDER FRUIT AND ITS CULTIVATION

In craft cider making there is a close relationship between the cider and the fruit. The grower and the cider maker are usually the same person, or if they are not then they work very closely together. In this chapter I will assume that to be the case and that the reader is intending to plant up a new cider orchard from scratch.

I will also assume some familiarity with the basics of apple cultivation, from existing practical experience or from one of the excellent textbooks on the subject – for instance those published by the Royal Horticultural Society. One of the best, now out of print but often available secondhand, is Harry Baker's *The Fruit Garden Displayed*. Michael Phillips' *The Apple Grower – a Guide for the Organic Orchardist* is an excellent American book. Cider orchards are not necessarily organic, but for various practical reasons they can often end up that way or at the very least as 'low input'.

Much of the detailed information in this chapter is specific to the British situation, since rootstocks and pests, for instance, differ markedly from country to country. Fruit grown in countries other than Britain is discussed at the end of the chapter.

CLASSIFICATION OF CIDER FRUIT

I mentioned previously that there is a great deal of merit in growing the dedicated cider varieties, and anyone planting up an orchard for cider use should certainly consider doing so. In practice, in the UK we are talking of a range of varieties grown traditionally in the West Country and the West Midlands. When the Long Ashton Cider Institute was founded in 1903 one of its first jobs was to classify the multitude of cider apples available. It quickly became apparent that this could be done on the basis of their acid and tannin levels, and hence Professor B.T.P. ('Bertie') Barker devised the grouping into four classes which we still use today. Barker was not alone in this – a similar system was also devised in France for the classification of Norman and Breton varieties, many of which are similar in composition.

Classification of Cider Apples

Class	Acid per cent	Tannin per cent
Sharp	> 0.45	< 0.2
Bittersharp	> 0.45	> 0.2
Bittersweet	< 0.45	> 0.2
Sweet	< 0.45	< 0.2

The most distinctive apples were the bittersweets and bittersharps, which possessed a tannin component which regular dessert apples lacked. Sometimes this tannin was 'hard' or bitter; sometimes it was 'soft' or astringent. We now understand the chemical reasons for this difference, which is essentially down to the size of the tannin (procyanidin) molecules. The larger

The Composition of Apple Juice *(figures in per cent by weight)*				
Component	Bramley	Cox	Typical bittersweet	'Ideal' cider apple
Sugar*	10	12	15	15
Malic acid	> 1	0.6	< 0.2	0.4
Tannin	< 0.05	0.1	> 0.2	0.2
Amino nitrogen	0–300 parts per million depending on cultivation			
Starch	0–2 per cent, depending on fruit maturity			
Pectin	0–1 per cent, depending on fruit storage period			
*The sugar proportions are typically fructose (70 per cent), glucose + sucrose (30 per cent).				

tannins are more astringent and the smaller ones are more bitter, and this is a characteristic of the actual fruit variety. Hence 'Tremletts Bitter' is always more bitter than 'Dabinett', even though their tannin levels are about the same. Overall, the presence of the tannin gives a richness and body to the cider which other apples lack; most modern dessert apples are very low in tannin.

Composition of the juice

About 80 per cent of the apple is water soluble in the form of juice. The approximate composition of that juice in different varieties is shown in the box. For a high quality craft cider in the West Country or French style, the composition of the 'ideal' cider juice should be similar to the figures in the last column. (For an Eastern Counties or German style, the acid would be somewhat higher, maybe up to 0.7 per cent, and the tannin lower).

Single or a blend?

Unfortunately very few 'true' cider apples actually match up to the ideal so in practice, a blend of cider apples is nearly always necessary. A renowned cultivar that does come close to the ideal is the bittersharp 'Kingston Black', but that tree often has poor orchard performance. So it is more usual to plant a range of bittersweet varieties using 'sharps' or to cull dessert apples to balance the acidity or, in commercial practice, to use 'Bramley' which always seems to be readily available.

For high quality craft cider a blend of apples is actually the norm. Do not be fooled by the modern fashion for so-called single varietal ciders on the supermarket shelves – most of them have been 'ameliorated' by adjustment to their tannin and acid levels to make them more consumer-friendly. Most true single varietal ciders are very unbalanced.

VINTAGE QUALITY

In addition to the figures shown, there is another elusive characteristic which can only be described as 'vintage quality', a term introduced by Hogg in the late nineteenth century and later popularized by Barker. There is no clear understanding of what this means in chemical terms –

A newly planted standard orchard protected against rabbits, hares and deer.

it is probably due to minute amounts of certain flavour precursors or possibly the presence of micronutrients which cause the fermentation yeast and bacteria to act in particular ways.

One fairly clear correlation seems to be that vintage quality trees take up less nitrogen from the soil and therefore the juices ferment more slowly.

Another general observation is that late-maturing cultivars, with fruit that stores well, tend to be of higher vintage quality than those which mature earlier. Indeed, the French traditionally divide their cider apples into three seasons of use, and consider those of the *troisième saison*, which do not mature until December or January, as being the very best for cider.

Overall, there is general agreement that certain cultivars produce a superior quality of cider to others, even though they may not give the highest yields, or may not be the easiest to grow.

Terroir

Of course soil type and climate can also play a major role. This is the concept of 'terroir'. An apple successful in one area may perform indifferently in another, even within the same county. For instance Hogg in *The Apple and Pear as Vintage Fruits* (1886) quotes 'Foxwhelp' as producing its finest ciders on deep sandstone soils of the Gloucestershire and Herefordshire river valleys whereas 'Forest Styre' produced its finest ciders on the thin upland limestones of the Forest of Dean only a few miles away. Both varieties performed indifferently when the situations were reversed.

True cider apples

Conversely, not all 'true' cider apples necessarily produce 'vintage quality.' The cultivar

Vintage Quality Cider Apple Cultivars

Name	Growing Habit	Flowers	Harvest	Comments
Sharp				
Frederick	Growth moderate, light crop, drooping and awkwardly placed growth. Susceptible to canker.	Early/mid	Mid Oct	Very fruity and characteristic high quality, but may not store long.
Brown's Apple	Vigorous, tends to biennialism. Scab resistant. Susceptible to canker and mildew.	Mid/late	End Oct	Fruity aroma.
Crimson King	Large triploid. Scab susceptible.	Mid	Mid Oct	Large fruits but better for cider than Bramley.
Mild bittersharp				
Kingston Black	Growth and cropping moderate. Slow to start bearing. Susceptible to scab and canker.	Mid	Mid Oct	Excellent distinctive flavour, allegedly the 'perfect' cider apple!
Medium bittersharp				
Broxwood Foxwhelp	Growth moderate, biennial.	Early	Sept/Oct	Full body and good acidic blender. Fruity aroma persists long after fermentation.
Dymock Red	Moderate, spreading, biennial.	Early	Sept/Oct	Good all round bittersharp.
Stoke Red	Slow and very twiggy. Resistant to scab, highly susceptible to mildew.	Mid/late	End Oct	Fruity aroma, high quality, for single variety cider or blending.

Name	Growing Habit	Flowers	Harvest	Comments
Medium bittersweet				
Dabinett	Small tree, precocious but grows neatly. Needs high potash. Susceptible to scab, mildew and canker.	Mid/late	End Oct/Nov	Soft but full-bodied tannin. A 'must have' for behaviour and blending! Less biennial than many.
Major	Growth spreading. Annual cropper. Slightly susceptible to scab, canker and silverleaf.	Mid	End Sept	Excellent soft tannin.
Yarlington Mill	Tends to droop. Good but biennial cropper. Scab susceptible.	Mid	Nov	Good light aromatic cider with soft tannin.
Full bittersweet				
Ashton Brown Jersey	Moderate growth, spurs well. Good yields but biennial.	Mid/late	Nov	Pronounced hard tannin.
Harry Masters Jersey	Compact, good annual cropper . Scab susceptible.	Mid/late	End Oct/Nov	High sugar, high tannin but fruit may not store.
Medaille d'Or	Smallish tree, wood brittle and tends to split. Strongly biennial.	Very late but self-fertile	End Oct/Nov	Very high but soft tannin.
Sweet				
Sweet Alford (not Le Bret)*	Strong annual cropper, tip-bearer and prone to scab.	Mid	End Oct	High sugar, good bulk for fermentation.
Sweet Coppin	Strong large tree. Mildew and scab susceptible and very biennial.	Mid	End Oct	Good all round sweet.

* Much 'Sweet Alford' in cultivation is actually mis-named and is really 'Le Bret'.

'Michelin', which is widely planted for cider making in Hereford and Somerset, is a good example of this. As a sort of 'Golden Delicious' of the cider world it is easy to grow and to process, but provides mere bulk without any distinction. A list of high quality cider vintage quality cultivars is shown in the box.

Traditional and recent cultivars

These apples are not ancient, most of them dating from the mid to late nineteenth century (although 'Foxwhelp' was well known as far back as the seventeenth century), but they have been well proven over the last 100 years or so. In the eighteenth century many other cider apples were renowned such as 'Herefordshire Redstreak' and 'Hagloe Crab,' but these have either been lost or do not appear to justify their former reputation. Anyone wanting to know more about the wide range of cider apples and their properties should consult Liz Copas' *Cider Apples*, the Marcher Apple Network CD *Vintage Cider Apples* or (for France) Boré and Fleckinger's *Pommiers à Cidre.*

It is worth noting that new cider apples were bred in the UK in recent years by Ray Williams and Liz Copas at the Long Ashton Research Station before its closure. They crossed Dabinett and Michelin with James Grieve and Worcester Pearmain, and some of these selections have recently been commercially released under a range of girls' names such as 'Lizzy' and 'Angela'. However, they were selected for early season cropping in modern intensive commercial pro-duction and not with the craft cider maker in mind, so it is not clear how many, if any, could be regarded as being of 'vintage quality' and suitable for low-input systems. But anyone of a curious disposition and who has the time and resources could plant them and find out – the information would certainly be valuable.

If you live in an area such as Gloucestershire or Dorset where long-lost native varieties have been rediscovered and are now being propa-gated in formal collections, you may want to try some of those. But for reliable high quality cider, those on the list shown here are known to be a good bet, even outside the traditional cider areas. For instance, in my own small orchard in South Oxfordshire I planted eleven cultivars from the list which have happily produced balanced and prizewinning ciders. However, on my thin chalk soils the cider is far less rich and intense than it might be on the deeper soils where those varieties originated. If things do not work out on your site you can always 'top-work' over the poor varieties to the better ones in later years.

Please do bear in mind the ultimate blend of fruit you will need – a cider made entirely from heavy bittersweets may have insufficient acid and too much tannin to produce good cider. One reason for my selection of eleven cultivars (four bittersweets, three sharps, two bitter-sharps, two sweets) was to be able to blend and ferment the juices all at one time in mid-season

Three top-worked 'rind grafts' in their third season.

to give a balanced cider. Remember also considerations like the fruit harvesting period. Few small cider makers can have a need for the early bittersweet cultivar 'Nehou', for instance, whose fruit is ready in late August but which bruises easily and does not store and at a time when there are few other apples to blend it with.

For a small plot or garden, where you have room for only a couple of trees, Dabinett and/or Yarlington Mill are an excellent bet because they are well-behaved and because you can almost certainly scrump or scrounge surplus acidic or dessert apples from friends and neighbours to produce a balanced juice for fermentation.

but they act as hosts to the 'fireblight' bacterium *Erwinia amylovora* which sometimes affects cider plantations. However, if the hedges are well laid and trimmed they will not flower so much and the risk can be minimized. Poplars are no longer recommended as windbreaks since they are too invasive, and *Leylandii* are too wind opaque, which causes turbulence and can even lead to trees being blown over rather than protected.

After the orchard is established and the trees well anchored it may become possible to remove all or part of the windbreak depending on local conditions. (I removed my willow windbreak after about fifteen years because it was becoming too large and was no longer necessary.)

THE ORCHARD

Location and shelter

For orchard location the same considerations apply as with dessert apples. Check that the soil is suitable, of appropriate pH and does not suffer from a deficiency of minerals such as magnesium. A soil analysis (for example, by the RHS) is a worthwhile investment so that problems can be corrected before planting. Cider apples tend to flower late so frost is not usually a problem, although overt frost pockets are best avoided. Ensure that all your trees will find a pollen partner locally by matching flowering times, or plant a few species *Malus* crabs as pollinators to ensure this.

Depending on exposure, a windbreak might be useful, certainly in the formative years. For a small site, fast growing willows such as *Salix* 'Bowles hybrid' will reach 12ft in three years when planted from cuttings through black polythene and can be trimmed annually or on a rotation thereafter. For larger orchards alder *Alnus cordata* provides an attractive and efficient fast-growing screen. Hawthorn hedges are effective

Spacing and yield

Tree size is an important consideration. Many people nowadays go for a semi-intensive bush orchard, for example on MM106 rootstock at 12–15ft spacing or on the dwarfer M26 at 8–12ft spacing. These trees should start to bear after three or four years and will bear fully from Year 10 onwards. If you take a longer term view and you have space for a truly traditional orchard as a landscape feature, you might like to go for standard trees on M25 spaced 30–40ft apart. They may take a decade to come into bearing but will go on for a century thereafter. In some parts of the country grant aid for planting new 'traditional' orchards may be available under various landscape and environmental schemes.

Allowing for overcrowding

If the trees grow well they may crowd each other to the extent that thinning and tree removal may be required after ten years or so. To allow for this it is worth initially planting on a 'quincunx' arrangement – that is, staggered rows so that each tree appears to be at the centre of a group of five. If thinning is required, alternate rows are removed to leave a resultant square pattern. Try this out on a sheet of squared paper and bear in mind that in a mixed orchard some cultivars at maturity may be different sizes. For instance, Crimson King on the same rootstock is about twice the size of Dabinett. So try to keep trees of the same type together for ease of later management. Although in theory this may affect pollination performance by bees, this is unlikely to be an issue except in very large orchards where separate pollinator varieties are sometimes planted in amongst otherwise identical groups. Most small cider growers will take for granted adequate pollination by bees and other insects, but if you can arrange for a hive to be present at blossom time this will certainly do no harm.

Yield

A reasonable yield for cider trees is an average of 5 tons per acre, but this can vary hugely due to biennial bearing ('on' one year and 'off' the next) and to the extent of fertilizer application. In commercial cider orchards nitrogen and potassium are applied annually, perhaps with the addition of phosphate and magnesium. The actual levels required are often determined by leaf and soil analysis.

For high quality cider it is undesirable to feed the trees more than is absolutely necessary and it is particularly important not to apply excess nitrogen. Yield may go up but quality certainly comes down and there is ample evidence that the best ciders are produced from apples low in nutrients (around 100 ppm of amino nitrogen in the table). Aim to keep your trees just healthy, but not in the 'lap of luxury'. For the small grower a light top dressing of established trees with Vitax every couple of years may be sufficient.

TREES

Obtaining the stock and planting it follows normal orcharding practice. However, there are only a few specialist nurseries selling cider trees and you may have to wait for them to be grafted or budded to order onto the rootstock you want, unless you have the skill to do it yourself and have access to the scions you require.

It is always best to start with maiden trees so you can train them properly from the start. Make sure you get virus-tested EMLA rootstocks and scions where they are available. Although traditional orchards might have been virus-ridden there seems little point in repeating this aspect of tradition now that healthy stock is available.

Planting the orchard

Received wisdom has it that trees should be pit-planted individually with plenty of organic matter and bonemeal and that good preparation is never wasted. However an alternative school of thought now recommends that 'luxury pits' do the tree more longer term harm than good, preventing it from establishing properly into the surrounding ground (see the Thornhayes Nursery website).

Trees will need good stakes and rabbit/hare guards, certainly for the first few years of life. It is now generally believed that high staking is undesirable because the stem should be allowed to flex in the wind to develop a firm and resilient structure – hence low staking, just above the graft union is now recommended. Some people further argue that on windy sites the trees should not be staked at all because the wind pressure causes stronger stems and more extensive roots to develop. However, not all growers agree with this and regard it as only applicable to forest

A newly staked tree in a protective wire mesh cage. The tie could with advantage be a little lower; the excess stake above the tie needs to be removed to prevent chafing.

trees, not to orchards. Wind rock can be a serious setback to firm tree establishment and can lead to a permanently weakened anchorage.

Floor

The best orchard floor is grass, although the immediate base of the trees should be kept clear of vegetation, certainly in the early years. Herbicides or special tree mats are used for this. If sowing a new sward, a slow growing mixture of chewings fescue (60 per cent) and brown-top bent (40 per cent) has been recommended,

or a slow-growing perennial ryegrass (sports turf mix) may be used. Some growers like to add white clover for its nitrogen fixing abilities. Specialist seedsmen now supply orchard floor mixes of slow growing grasses and wild herbs.

In a new 'traditional' orchard of standard trees there may be enough space for wildflowers to be established in the alleyways. Spring flowering woodland edge species such as primrose, bluebell, cowslip, ladies' smock and red campion are best for this since the sward will inevitably require cutting during the summer. The grass should be cut as frequently as required, with the mowings allowed to rot *in situ* or used as a mulch at the base of the trees. Grass should never be removed from the orchard because this can lead to severe potassium deficiency and subsequent tree defoliation. A final grass cut can be made just prior to harvest so that the fruit has a short, clean sward on which to fall.

Muntjac deer damage to mature tree bark.

You can run livestock such as sheep in traditional orchards, although the tree trunks must be well protected by fencing. This is more difficult in bush orchards since both trunks and lower branches are vulnerable to browsing. As the trees mature, however, the lower tier of branches can be removed to allow for grazing if required, though the trunks will still need protection – it is not uncommon to see old plastic fertilizer sacks pressed into service. Chickens or geese are an alternative to sheep in dwarf orchards (and chickens greatly enjoy the blossoms on the lower branches). Livestock should always be removed a minimum of fifty-six days before harvest to reduce the risk of bacterial contamination of fruit by animal droppings, as specified in NACM/DEFRA advice. As a hobbyist, I do not actually remove my chickens but I certainly do wash my fruit thoroughly.

PRUNING AND MANAGEMENT

Pruning of bush cider trees is rather different from that of dessert apples. There is no need to go for the 'open goblet' shape or the pruning of laterals – in fact pruning can be fairly minimal. Fruit size and finish is not tremendously important, and hard pruning of most cider varieties tends to stimulate excessive growth and can encourage biennial bearing.

Shape

Current commercial practice favours a 'hedgerow wall' with a dominant centre leader, which is really designed for convenience during spraying and mechanical harvesting of the fruit. For the smaller grower the objective should still be to maintain a good central leader with fruitful side branches as near horizontal as possible, although not all cultivars will respond equally readily to this ideal. One of the great virtues offered by a centre leader pattern is the excellent light penetration that a triangular tree affords which promotes maximum efficiency and productivity and helps reduce biennialism.

However, it takes some work to keep it in shape as a mature tree, and many of the more traditional cultivars tend to revert to a more spreading pattern if annual management input is skipped or insufficient. In my own little orchard I confess to being considerably at fault in this respect!

Pruning guidance

At planting, prune the maiden tree to a good bud about 3ft above ground level, rubbing out the two buds below as they break in spring. Existing side branches ('feathers') below 2ft should be cut off flush with the stem, but those above 2ft may be retained as part of the first tier of permanent branches. In subsequent springs the leader may be tipped slightly back to a good growth bud, and the two buds below should be rubbed out. This will help more horizontal laterals to break further down and reduce competition with the leader.

During the summer branches that do begin to compete vigorously with the leader should be cut out. Do not allow more than two side branches per 4 inches vertical run of stem. In autumn it will be worth tying down any upward pointing side-branches to a more horizontal position. Not only will this increase their fruitfulness by reducing their vigour, but by developing wide branch angles it will prevent them splitting under heavy loads when carrying fruit later.

In later years, once the tree structure is established, pruning consists mainly of removing damaged or crowded branches so that light and air can get to all parts of the tree and the structure can be maintained.

For standard trees there is less formative management and the maidens are allowed to grow on without pruning. They are headed back once they have reached 6ft or so, and the crown is allowed to develop more or less naturally. However, it has also been demonstrated that a budded standard tree (not a grafted one where the buds break sideways) can be trained in centre leader form, which combines both landscape value and productivity.

Pests and diseases

Pests and diseases of cider trees are similar to those of dessert fruit, although the severity of attacks may be less. Codling moth and other types of caterpillar damage are scarcely important to the cider maker unless extremely severe and even large cider growers may only spray routinely against scab and mildew. Some indication of disease susceptibility is given in the table of apple varieties. There is some evidence that seaweed extract (Maxicrop) may improve the tree's resistance to mildew and scab attack. Frequently, no spraying at all is required and cider apples are therefore well suited to organic cultivation.

Fireblight

Fireblight, though, is a potential problem and is spread from blossom to blossom in spring by pollinating insects which carry the bacterium. In the south of England this may become more of a problem in future years as climate change advances. There is no easy solution short of vigilant and constant monitoring – affected limbs and shoots should be cut out and burnt as soon as the disease is noted. Young apples and perry pear trees are particularly susceptible. In many parts of the US, fireblight is often endemic and can be a serious problem for people trying to grow non-resistant European cider varieties such as Yarlington Mill and Harry Masters Jersey.

Biennial bearing

Biennial bearing is perhaps the biggest single headache for the cider grower. It is caused by a large crop in one year (the 'on' year) suppressing flower-bud formation for the next year (the 'off' year). This pattern is often set by external climatic factors, such as a warm summer, so that all the trees in a locality tend to go 'in phase' with each other. For the UK as a whole there is a strong biennial trend. For instance, crops in the years 1980, '82 and '84 were about twice those in 1981, '83 and '85.

There are various remedies for biennial bearing, mostly using hormone sprays to control flower bud initiation, or even using hand removal of part of the blossom in an 'on' year to ensure some crop in the subsequent 'off' year. Carbaryl was an effective hormonal spray but is no longer permitted under EU directives due to its potentially adverse environmental effects and toxicity to birds, insects and mammals. There are no hormonal fixes for biennial bearing at present.

Most good growers are able to keep crops coming by a combination of stress-free and competition-free (weeds and grass) tree growth, good renewal pruning practice done every other year at least and a modicum of NPK. The key is to maintain a balance between adequate vegetative growth and fruiting. For large manufacturers, this problem has been considerably reduced in recent years by the choice of less biennial cultivars such as Dabinett and Michelin, and by the production of apple juice concentrate which is made and used as an ingredient 'in house'. This not only smooths out the biennial cropping cycles but also enables cider to be made more evenly throughout the year.

OLD ORCHARDS

If you have acquired or inherited an existing mature or derelict orchard then you may be lucky indeed. Not only may it contain unique local varieties, it may also be rich in wildlife such as beetles, owls and woodpeckers. Here there is a balance to be struck between commercial productivity on the one hand and wildlife and landscape interest on the other. Expert advice should be sought from your County Wildlife Trust or Farming and Wildlife Advisory Group (FWAG). It is usually possible to take a reasonable fruit crop while maintaining the orchard's biodiversity.

Replanting

Partial replanting may not be a good option, though, since apple trees do not generally thrive where apples have grown before, unless all the old soil surrounding the roots is removed and fresh soil put in its place. (Be careful though not to create a 'sump' of lighter material such as peat or manure, which holds water too tenaciously and does not drain away through heavy soil.) In this case strong varieties like Yarlington Mill gap-up well, while Dabinett – a smaller and weaker variety – gets too easily daunted when surrounded by large old trees.

Rejuvenation

Top-working, or grafting a preferred new variety onto an older mature tree which has been cut back, may sometimes be a better route. Derelict trees can often be restored on a thinning and pruning programme spread out over three years; it is not done all at once since this is too much of a shock to the system and will result either in dead trees or in excessive and uncontrolled re-growth ('water sprouts').

Mistletoe is often found in old orchards; too much can weaken the tree.

If you have acquired an existing orchard of predominantly dessert or culinary fruit rather than bittersweets, the cider made from it may be rather acid to your taste. Top-working some trees over to bittersweet varieties is a possible and longer-term answer to this problem. However, it is now possible to reduce the acidity of the finished cider by using malo-lactic bacterial cultures, an approach which is covered in a later chapter.

There is no need to act hastily with an inherited orchard. Observe and live with it for a couple of seasons and take plenty of advice (albeit often conflicting!) before deciding what to do.

A Kingston Black tree with most of its fruit shed on the ground.

Using a long 'panking' pole to dislodge the remaining fruit.

HARVESTING

Cider fruit should never be harvested until it is fully ripe, and in the UK and France it is usual for much of the crop to fall on the ground before harvesting commences – the tree can be shaken or poked with long sticks (panking poles) to bring down the rest. This is very different from the careful harvesting of dessert apples, and harvesting from the ground may be regarded as a bizarre or even an illegal practice in other parts of the world. However, because

Collecting fruit from the orchard floor.

Plastic buckets are ideal for carrying apples.

the fermentation step of cidermaking destroys any pathogens that may transfer to the apples from ground contamination, this is an entirely safe practice.

Large growers use tractor-mounted tree shakers, air blowers and mechanical brushes to sweep up the fruit from the orchard alley-ways. This can cause some fruit damage, but a small amount of bruising is usually acceptable. Smaller growers will usually be hand-harvesting using buckets and barrows, or hand-operated mechanical harvesters of the 'Tuthill' type or the SFM 'Grouse'. Spiked-roller harvesters ('hedge-hogs') should never be used because the tines penetrate the fruit which leads to inoculation with undesirable soil micro-organisms and acts as a focus for mould growth.

For very small scale use, the 'Apple Wizard' is a clever hand-held device which was originally developed for harvesting fallen pecan nuts in the US but is sold in the UK for cider apple collection. It works best if the ground is even and the grass fairly closely mown.

Apple Wizard ready for work.

Apple Wizard collecting fruit.

Transfer to the collection tub.

The spike opens the wires and the fruit falls out.

Operation completed.

A small barrow can move fruit boxes efficiently.

Storage before pressing

The fruit should ideally be harvested into slatted wooden or plastic boxes for storage so that air can circulate. Polypropylene or jute sacks, even of an open weave, are not satisfactory for storage for more than a day or two since the fruit will sweat, although in large operations wooden and concrete silos are used.

Once harvested, mid- to late-season fruit need not be processed at once. It has traditionally been considered necessary to store the fruit up to a month or so after harvesting. The major reason for this is that starch in the fruit is still being converted into sugar even once the fruit is off the tree and it is desirable that this process should be complete before fermentation. Changes in flavour precursors also probably occur. However, soluble pectin is also produced as the fruit is stored which may eventually cause problems of sliminess when the fruit is being pressed. So it is unwise to store the fruit for too long – two to four weeks is probably a reasonable period.

As with dessert apples, early maturing

Bagged fruit ready for milling. (Photo: Ray Blockley)

varieties are best processed almost immediately since they do not store well. Traditionally the apples are ready for milling when they retain the impression of a thumbprint after squeezing in the hand. A slightly more scientific approach is to use a commercial iodine solution dropped onto the freshly cut fruit surface, the presence of unchanged starch showing as a blue stain.

A drop of iodine solution is placed on the cut fruit surface. Unripe fruit (top) stains black; ripe fruit (below) remains pale yellow.

Fruit stack elevated off the ground to provide some protection against rodents and birds.

If fruit is to be stored, especially outdoors, it will need protection from pests such as rats, squirrels and even otherwise friendly blackbirds. Fruit in storage should be inspected frequently and any rotten or mouldy fruit discarded. Some bruising is acceptable and inevitable due to the method of harvesting, but it is at the bruise sites where mould may start to grow, especially if the skin is broken.

CIDER APPLES OUTSIDE NORTHERN EUROPE

Until recent years, it was really only in the UK, France and Spain that special cider apples were grown with no alternative use as table apples, although in countries with a long cider history, such as the US, there are some 'heritage' varieties such as Hewes Virginia Crab or Harrison which have been primarily grown for cider. While it is certainly possible to grow the European cider varieties in many parts of the New World, there are a couple of caveats to be aware of.

Naming

One of these caveats is sourcing and naming. For instance most if not all cider varieties currently available in the US and Australia were imported many years ago into just a few nurseries and national collections before modern plant health restrictions and quarantine made it the much more complex and regulated process that it is today.

For reasons now lost to history, a few of the varieties in the US are known to be misnamed; for instance the US Foxwhelp is nothing like the true UK Foxwhelp at all, and the US Tremletts Bitter is more of a bittersharp than the heavy bittersweet it should be. Not all US Yarlington Mill is the true variety. There is an apple known in the US as Hagloe Crab but it bears no relationship to any British Hagloe Crab. So the buyer must beware. In Australia the situation is somewhat better and many of the British and French cider varieties available have also been verified against authentic stock in their country of origin.

Climate

A second consideration is growth conditions and climate. Generally speaking, the warmer the growing conditions for a specific variety, the lower the acid and tannin levels and the higher the sugar. I have drunk Kingston Black ciders grown and made in central California (US) and Victoria (Australia) which were very high in alcohol (9 per cent) and were unrecognizable as Kingston Black in UK terms due to their low acid and low tannin. So, if you live in a climate very different from those in which the cider apples originated, you may find that the cider you make from them is quite different too.

In hot areas, the fruit may also be prone to issues such as sunburn and water core. On the other hand, European cider apples grown in the cooler damper conditions of the Pacific Northwest (coastal Washington and British Columbia, for instance) will perform similarly to the way they do at home. Conversely, some European cider varieties such as Medaille d'Or and Stoke Red will not perform adequately in the cold winters and short growing seasons of Québec, nor in the mountain climate of Colorado. Paradoxically, many northern European apples do have a specific requirement for a certain period of winter chill or their fruit set and leaf cover will be poor. This has been a problem in the warmer parts of southern Australia such as Victoria but less so in the highland areas of New South Wales. Dabinett and Stoke Red in particular crop poorly in Australia for this reason.

This is not to dissuade anyone from trying to grow European cider varieties in the New World. But understand what you are planning to do, and be prepared to experiment. There may also be 'heritage' varieties in your own area which would be worth trying. It is wise to consult with local cider growers and enthusiasts before embarking on a large-scale planting programme.

3 JUICING AND FERMENTING

This chapter is about a key step in the cider making process: preparing the juice and fermenting it to a fully dry cider. For this you will need to have the ripe fruit, the mill and the press all set up and with plenty of clean containers for pulp and juice to hand. The exact details will vary depending on your set-up, but the fundamentals remain the same. If you have a mixture of fruit to work with, say sharps and bittersweets, which are intended to produce a balanced final blend as described in Chapter 2, it is generally a much better plan to mill and ferment mixed loads than it is to focus on just one variety at a time. The reason for that is primarily to do with control of pH and prevention of microbial infection, as described later.

Discarded fruit not fit for cider making!

FRUIT WASHING

Before milling, fruit should be washed to remove soil, dead insects, leaves, stones and rotten apples. It is fortunate that healthy apples float in water (pears do not!), thus providing an easy way to wash and clean the fruit. It is amazing how much dirt and mud collects at the bottom of a washing tank. Rotten apples should be discarded – a good rule of thumb is that if you would not willingly eat it then do not make cider from it. A little bruising is quite acceptable and inevitable though. Some craft cider makers make a feature of cutting out damaged portions from every single apple, but this is very time consuming and personally I have never found it necessary.

Washing system

The washing system you use will depend on your local circumstances, but some sort of large sink or tub which can be refilled with clean water is required, ideally with a slatted basket or some easy way to remove the rinsed fruit. Many types of wide plastic tub, preferably 'food grade', can be pressed into service. For instance you can use a cut-down IBC plastic tank filled with water and a plastic garden rake to agitate and to remove the washed apples. A hose with a spray jet makes it easier to remove compacted mud.

When the water gets too dirty – change it. If the water is recycled too often, the dirt is

Apple washing in a cut-down IBC. (Photo: Ray Blockley)

Turning the washing apples.

Removing apples from the wash.

(where the flower petals once were). However, these yeasts (species such as *Kloeckera* and *Candida*) have only weak fermenting power and they soon die in more than a couple of per cent of alcohol. They are not the *Saccharomyces* yeasts which are required for the successful completion of fermentation. In a traditional cider-making operation where no yeast is apparently used, the *Saccharomyces* inoculum resides on the press racks, the cloths, the vats, or even on the walls and ceiling. It persists from season to season but virtually none of it comes directly from the apples. We will discuss yeasts and the benefits of using wild or cultured strains in more detail later.

MILLING

The exact procedure for milling and pressing will depend on the equipment you have. For a typical pack press set-up, the pulp produced by the mill should be individual chunks or shreds each about the diameter of a pea – smaller than that and you may end up with apple purée squeezing through the cloths when you press; larger than that and you will not extract the juice from the cells efficiently, so yields will be low. The commercially available electrically powered mills are designed to produce pulp of the right size. For some years I used a second-hand grape crusher which was not really the right tool for the job and all the pulp had to be processed twice to get it to the right size. Before that I used a 6ft length of heavy 6-inch square ash timber, pounding the apples in a wooden trough, which was even less efficient.

Modern mills are fitted with safety cut-outs so it should not be possible to gain access inside while the blades are running. If a mill jams on a large fruit, or from too rapid a feed rate, it is usually best to stop the mill, unplug it, and clear the blockage by hand. Sometimes the judicious

A good working height.

recycled too. Some cidermakers use a two-stage washing, dumping the apples into one tub for a first quick rough cleaning and inspection, then into a second tub for the final wash. This cuts down on the interval between water changes. It is generally worthwhile arranging the washing station at work-table height, since constant bending or squatting quickly gets to be quite miserable. On a cold winter's day fruit washing is not the most pleasant of jobs, but good water-proof gloves and an apron make the job slightly more bearable. A friend to help and to chat to is a useful accessory too.

Do not be afraid of washing away the yeast. It is a popular fallacy that desirable fermenting yeasts are present on the fruit skin. There are indeed some types of yeast on the skin and in fact there can be as many as 50,000 yeast cells per gram of fruit actually inside the apple itself, which probably get there through the open eye

Fresh pulp from a Speidel mill.

Milled pulp quickly browns on top. (Photo: Ray Blockley)

use of a wooden pusher or broom handle can clear a blockage without the need for stripping down. You will soon learn the idiosyncrasies and peculiarities of your own mill, and they all have them!

The milled pulp is usually discharged to a plastic hopper or maybe a wheeled stainless steel bin. Once apples are milled, the pulp is surprisingly dense and packs down to about half the volume of the original fruit, so you do not want to be moving the containers of pulp any further than you have to. Generally the pulp is pressed as soon as it is milled, with some exceptions which will be mentioned later. You may notice that the pulp oxidizes or browns very rapidly on top but may stay quite colourless underneath

where air cannot penetrate. You may also notice curious wasps, which can be quite a nuisance early in the season.

PRESSING

Setting up

Most craft cidermakers will be using a pack (or 'rack and cloth') press, which is a design tried and tested over many hundreds of years. To start the process, a wooden or plastic rack is laid on the press bed/juice tray, and then a wooden or

A home-made press with net curtains as cloths; no racks are being used here. (Photo: Ray Blockley)

metal frame or 'form' about 2 inches high is set squarely on the rack. A press cloth is laid in the form such that its corners protrude from each side of the square (typically, a rack 18 inches square would need a 16-inch square form and cloths 30 inches square). Commercial press cloths are nowadays made from coarsely woven polyester or similar fabric, but for a home-made press a fair and cheap substitute is given by a length of plain weave nylon 'net curtain' material from a drapery store. Various other types of synthetic fibre mesh (polyethylene or polypropylene) can also be pressed into service, for instance those used in horticulture or even in the building trade.

Pulp

Pulp is then scooped into the cloth and distributed evenly to the height of the form. The cloth sides are then folded over alternately to form a neat envelope of pulp. The form is removed, a new rack is added on top of the 'cheese' just formed and the process is repeated. Typically a pack press will contain ten or a dozen cheeses, maybe more (though it is a moot point whether the word 'cheese' refers to an individual parcel of pulp as I have just described, or to the whole assemblage). It is important that the pulp layers be uniform and to check that the stack is vertical, not leaning.

Laying the pulp in a cloth on a Voran press.

Filling the form.

Completing the stack.

Folding the cloth.

Once the stack is complete a spare rack is placed on the top of the stack and the pressure is applied. In some designs the cheese(s) can be built up away from the press plate and then wheeled into position for pressing, thus making it easier to work. Pressure may be applied by hand

Rolling the stack into position.

Juice flowing under pressure.

(usually from above, if a screw thread or bottle jack design), or by electric power if a hydraulic ram design (from below, to prevent any leakage of hydraulic oil seeping into the juice).

Juices

All pack presses give some 'free-run' juice while the cheeses are being built and before any pressure is applied, so a collection vessel should be in place below the juice tray from the very beginning. It is convenient to have available two 25-litre plastic containers for this since 15kg or so is a reasonable load to carry to the fermenting vessel. A friend to help with this is very useful – indeed milling and pressing is most easily done as a two-person operation. Alternatively, it

Collection vessel in place under a home-made press.

An intermediate juice buffer tank gravity-fed from a two-bed Voran press; the contents are pumped direct to a fermentation tank.

is possible to rig up gravity-feed pipework to a small holding tank from which the juice is then pumped to the main fermentation tank.

Once maximum pressure is reached there is a 'law of diminishing returns' on how far you continue to press to get a little more juice, and how long you go on may rather depend on what else you have to do at the time. If you are using dessert fruit, rather than the more fibrous cider fruit, you may need to watch how much pressure you apply and to be sure not to let the pulp squeeze out through the cloth. In this case a long continued low pressure is better than a harder squeeze to get good juice yield without excessive solids, or pectolytic enzymes can be used on the pulp (see later).

Finishing off

Once pressing is finished the cheeses are stripped down and the press-cake or 'pomace' sheets are removed. They may be composted, spread evenly back in the orchard, or fed in small doses to livestock, but beware since they will start to ferment or go mouldy in a day or so. The pomace may also be converted to silage for animal feeding at a later date – in this case it is very tightly packed into black plastic silage bags and firmly sealed so that air is totally excluded. If correctly done the pomace will ensile sweetly without the need for any additives.

Depending on the efficiency of your press a fair amount of sugar may still remain in the dry pomace, so by adding a litre or two of water to each 5kg of broken-up pomace before re-pressing, a useful yield of slightly weaker juice may be obtained, which is usually added to the first pressing. As a rule of thumb there is little to be gained by doing this if your yield is 70 per cent or over, but with a home-made press it may be worthwhile. Some rough figures on press-type and efficiency are shown in the box.

Efficiency

Yield is not a linear function with pressure; it only increases by about 5 per cent with each doubling of the pressure. If possible it is worth aiming for a minimum 70 per cent juice yield and hence a minimum pressure of about 70 psi.

Part of the efficiency of a pack press derives from the multitude of thin layers and their separation by the racks and cloths; if there is no separation of the layers, the press is much less efficient. If you watch a press working you will see that each layer is in effect pressed

Dry pomace sheets after removal from press.

Press Type vs Efficiency

- My home-made wooden press with 16" effective square cheese and a 2-ton jack gave 120 kPa or 17 psi and a juice yield of about 60 per cent. This is a low yield and I often used to re-wet the pomace and re-press when I was using this jack, to improve the yield. This press took six cheeses and about 40kg of pulp per pressing.

- The same with an 8-ton jack gives 480 kPa or 70 psi and a juice yield around 70 per cent. Generally I did not find it was worth wetting and re-pressing the pomace once I was using this jack.

- My commercial Voran press (steel frame and electric hydraulics) gives 952 kPa or 138 psi, with a juice yield about 75 per cent. This press takes 9 × 18" cheeses and about 80kg of pulp per pressing.

HDPE sheets used as racks. (Photo: Ray Blockley)

independently of its neighbours, the juice escaping from each individual rack. (Even cloths on their own, without racks, provide some measure of separation, but it is generally believed that racks assist the flow of juice.)

Basket presses are inherently less efficient because they do not allow the juice to escape so easily. In a pack press it is important that there should be racks under the very bottom layer and at the very top to allow the juice to get away. I have heard of juice being forced into the wood of the press tray itself for lack of this precaution, the whole base becoming permeated with juice.

Although the wooden racks are traditionally of slatted construction it is not necessary that they be so, since the juice moves laterally along the easiest pathway and not downwards from rack to rack. Hence it is perfectly possible to use sealed plywood or HDPE (polythene) sheet instead of conventional racks to separate the layers of pulp. HDPE sheets of around 8mm

Juice running efficiently from each layer. (Photo: Ray Blockley)

Manual cleaning of wooden racks.

thickness may be bought cut to order and many people have found them very satisfactory and much easier to clean than wooden racks. It is not even necessary to groove or to route channels in these racks, although some people do.

People sometimes worry about crushing apple seeds during cider making because they have heard that they contain cyanide and fear that it may poison them. This is not a problem. It is true that apple seeds do contain cyanide in the form of amygdalin, a cyanogenic glucoside, but they contain about the same amount as almonds (another fruit seed). The seeds would have to be broken and a special enzyme which our bodies lack is also needed to liberate the cyanide. In practice very few seeds are actually broken as can be seen if the apple pomace is closely inspected. So the level of cyanide in apple juice or cider is tiny, a fraction of a part per million and way below any health concerns (the EU limit for cyanide in almonds and marzipan is 50 parts per million).

UNDERSTANDING THE FERMENTING PROCESSES

Sugar content and specific gravity

Until you have pressed out your juice you may not have much idea of its sugar content.

It is possible to press out single drops of juice from an apple by hand and measure its percentage sugar content with a 'field refractometer' as used by grape growers but these are expensive (about £50 for a budget model) and most people do not have one. Also they can only be used with juice, not on part-fermented cider, since the alcohol affects the refractometer reading.

The key measurement after pressing is sugar content by 'specific gravity' (SG) as measured with a hydrometer, which are easily and cheaply obtained from home brew shops. The SG of pure water is defined as 1.000 and the sugar in the juice raises the level. The table in the box, based on data obtained from French cider and

Specific Gravity vs Percent Sugar and Potential Alcohol

SG at 20°C	Per cent Sugar % w/v	Potential Alcohol % v/v
0.998	0.0	0.0
1.000	0.47	0.2
1.005	1.6	0.9
1.010	2.6	1.5
1.015	3.7	2.1
1.020	4.8	2.8
1.025	5.9	3.4
1.030	6.9	4.0
1.035	8.0	4.6
1.040	9.1	5.3
1.045	10.2	5.9
1.050	11.2	6.5
1.055	12.3	7.2
1.060	13.4	7.8
1.065	14.5	8.4
1.070	15.5	9.1

Note that for historical reasons the sugar figure is conventionally given in per cent weight/volume (grams per 100ml), whereas the alcohol level is conventionally expressed as per cent volume/volume (ml per 100ml).

It may seem slightly odd that the table goes down to SG 0.998. That is because the final SG of a fermented cider includes the contribution due to the alcohol whose SG is much lower than water at SG 0.789)

juices in the 1990s, gives SG, per cent sugar content and potential alcohol content (ABV or 'alcohol by volume') if all that sugar ferments out.

To read a hydrometer you need the hydrometer itself and a suitable tall jar or measuring cylinder for it to float in – it is more usual to draw off a sample for measurement rather than to immerse the hydrometer in the bulk liquid.

The temperature of the juice should also be at or close to the temperature for which it is calibrated (usually 15 or 20°C).

Jiggle the hydrometer up or down a few times and take the reading at the bottom of the meniscus when it has come to rest, making sure it is not resting on the wall of the jar.

When measuring fermenting cider, the gas bubbles stick to the hydrometer and can easily

A hydrometer being used to measure SG in a bulk juice tank. (Photo: Ray Blockley)

A hand-held refractometer. A drop of juice is placed on the glass prism and the cover is closed; the operator looks through the eyepiece towards the light and reads the sugar content on an internal scale.

give false readings, so you need to spin or jiggle the instrument quite vigorously several times to detach the gas bubbles. Alternatively, you can partially degas a cider sample by placing it in a microwave oven for a few seconds, or by pouring it repeatedly from one jar to another.

By measuring the SG at the beginning and end of the fermentation you can readily calculate the alcohol by difference, which is a great advantage since this is very difficult to measure without costly laboratory equipment. The alcohol level can be inferred from the table or you can just divide the gravity difference by 8 to get a fair figure (for example, 1.050 – 0.998 = 52, 52/8 = 6.5. The table also gives 6.5 per cent ABV for a juice of SG 1.050).

It is important to realize that all such data can only be approximate due to the inherent natural variability of apple composition. For any given SG value in the table, the alcohol yield could in practice be 0.3 per cent higher or lower than the mean figure quoted. Also, the cheap wide-range hydrometers used by most hobby cidermakers are not as accurately calibrated as the more expensive laboratory type, so the readings may not be 'spot on' in any case. However, for most purposes such high accuracy is not required.

You may sometimes see sugar levels referred to as 'degrees Brix', and many refractometers and some hydrometers are calibrated in this way. This is in theory the per cent of sugar in the juice by mass (weight). However, the refractometers are calibrated against pure sucrose, which apple juice is not, and its refractive index is dictated by things other than just sugars. So the true sugar content is lower than the simple Brix reading would imply; the same is true of a 'Brix hydrometer' too.

Sugar levels are set largely by the weather and it is actually the intensity of sunlight rather than the temperature that is the key factor. In a really good summer in the UK we might see sugar levels up to 15 per cent, but in a poorer summer less than 10 per cent might be achieved.

As a rule of thumb, if the juice SG is less than 1.045 and you have no sweeter juice for blending, it is wise to bring it up to this level by the addition of sugar. Otherwise the resultant alcohol may not be sufficient to protect the final cider during storage (this is the true meaning and intent of 'chaptalization'). To raise the SG in 5 degree steps, dissolve around 10 grams of sugar in each litre of juice and re-test with the hydrometer until the desired level is reached.

More problematic perhaps is what to do in a good year when the potential alcohol level might exceed 8.5 per cent (the UK legal limit) and when you are getting into 'apple wine' territory. The best plan is probably to ferment 'as is' and then think later whether you want or need to dilute the resultant cider. In practice it is an empirical fact that dilution of cider up to about 15 per cent (that is, 85 per cent juice equivalent) has little impact on flavour. So a fermented cider at 9 per cent alcohol could be taken back to 7.5 per cent with water without too much adverse effect. This is why the various suggested 'codes of practice' for craft cidermakers, who are fundamentally making full-juice ciders, do allow for some water dilution – it would be impossibly restrictive otherwise.

I would not generally suggest the addition of brown sugar, raisins, spices and similar ingredients to a cider. However, for North American readers it is worth pointing out that there is a venerable tradition of New England ciders which does involve fortifying the juice in this way before fermentation, and maybe adding rum or brandy and extra sugar afterwards to drive up the alcohol levels and to keep it sweet. In effect this is a form of flavoured apple wine for consumption by rural folk in intense cold winters, and who can blame them? In the less cold climate of Old England, mulled cider with sugar, spices and citrus can be very sustaining, especially at a January wassail in a frosty orchard. But recipes for flavoured cider are not the purpose of this book.

Measuring pH

At this point we need to measure the pH of the juice, which is actually controlled more by the variety of fruit than the climate, although weather and the degree of fruit ripeness do also play some role. A desirable juice pH range for cider making is say 3.3 to 3.8. At higher pH the fermentation will be subject to microbial infection and at pH 4.0 or above this can lead to serious flavour problems. Many traditional bittersweet cider apples tend to be high in pH which is why they need blending with more acid fruit, preferably before fermentation. That is also a reason why bittersharp apples, such as 'Kingston Black', have been regarded as close to perfection in terms of their composition for single-variety cider making. Conversely at low pH (<3.3), the acidity will be quite high so the final cider may be unacceptably sharp to the palate. Bramley juices for instance, often have a pH around 3.0, although if the fruit is kept in cold store for a few months before pressing the pH will rise and the acidity will drop as the fruit respires and metabolizes the acid.

Measurement of pH is best done by a dedicated 'pH meter'. Laboratory versions are expensive, costing several hundred pounds, but microchip technology has now brought 'dip-stick' pH meters for cider and winemakers down to as little as £20 or so. (Beware the very cheap pH meters which are sold in garden centres for soil testing – these are not accurate enough and do not cover the correct range for cider making).

pH meters do need some care in handling and they must be calibrated before each use with a suitable 'buffer solution' which can be purchased pre-prepared. For cider making a single point calibration at pH 4 is quite satisfactory

What is pH and What is Acidity?

It is helpful for the cidermaker to understand these two quantities and the differences between them, because although they are complementary they are not the same thing.

The pH is an inverse logarithmic measure of the concentration of free hydrogen ions in a chemical or biological system. It is a very important concept in cell biochemistry. A lot of processes like the growth of spoilage microbes and the effectiveness of sulphur dioxide are dependent on pH, so it is a very useful quantity to measure in juice before fermentation.

Titratable acid, on the other hand, is a simple measure of the (related) amount of acid 'anions' in a juice. In general, titratable acid (TA) relates pretty well to the 'acid taste' of a juice or cider. If the TA doubles, people will tend to perceive it as twice as acidic. So it is a useful quantity to measure if you are thinking of blending different types of apples, or blending finished ciders for taste after fermentation.

There is no direct relationship between titratable acidity and pH in apple juice, and all juices differ, although generally the pH goes up as the acid goes down and vice versa. Very roughly a dessert apple with a pH around 3.4 may have a TA around 0.7 per cent. And a bittersweet cider apple with a pH around 4.0 may have a TA of around 0.2 per cent. But you cannot measure one and accurately predict the other. You have to make two separate measurements.

since it is close to the pH of interest. The glass electrode, which is the 'business end' of the pH meter, must not be allowed to dry out and should be stored wet according to the manufacturer's directions. Cheaper pH meters do not have replaceable electrodes and may only last a season or two before the electrode becomes

**Measuring juice pH with a dipstick pH meter.
(Photo: Ray Blockley)**

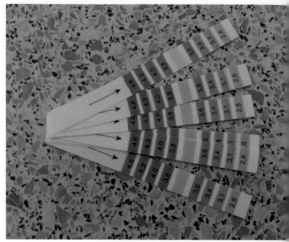

**The pH papers are dipped briefly into the juice,
and the colour in the centre panel is compared
with the pre-printed reference panels.**

sluggish and unusable. It may be best to regard them as effectively disposable after a couple of seasons. The better quality and more costly pH meters do have replaceable electrodes.

It is also possible to get a measurement of pH very cheaply using special pH test papers. A widely available commercial paper covers the range 2.8–4.6. To use the paper it is dipped briefly in the juice, and the colour in the middle bar is then compared for closest match with the adjacent colours on the pre-printed strip. Unfortunately tests on apple juice compared to pH meters have shown that they are not very accurate. However, if you are just starting out in cider making they will give you a reasonable idea of where you are. Also, due to the dyes which are used, experience shows that these strips only give the correct colour rendering in daylight or daylight quality artificial light (such as a halogen reading lamp). This is an important point since on a typical cider making day it may not be till dusk or later that you actually get to take the pH reading!

If the pH is below 3.8, there is no need to take any action. If the pH is above 3.8–4.0, you should really try to blend the juice with a more acid juice before fermentation. If that is not possible, an alternative is the addition of malic acid in steps of 1 gram per litre (0.1 per cent) until the pH is sufficiently reduced at least to below 4.0, preferably further. You might need up to 0.3 per cent addition. Malic acid is the natural acid in apples and is better for cider than citric acid. If the juice is already very acid, with a pH below 3.3, it will not adversely affect fermentation but it does indicate that the final cider will be quite acidic. If you have some higher pH juice available, you can blend it in now; or, if you know that you have other juice on the way which will provide a slightly less acid cider, you can wait to do that blending until after fermentation.

ADDITIONS

Let us assume that the juice is now blended in its fermenting vessel, with its SG measured and its pH known. There are a couple of additions we might consider.

Pectic enzyme and nutrients

If the juice has been made mostly from dessert apples and you found the pulp a bit gloopy and difficult to press, it might give you a pectin haze in the finished cider. So, if it is important that the final cider should be sparklingly clear, a pectolytic enzyme can be added at this stage, which will help to ensure that all the pectin is broken down. Pectin is a sort of natural glue which sticks the apple cell walls together. Although it is water-soluble it is precipitated by alcohol, so it tends to lead to persistent hazes by the end of fermentation.

Dessert fruit, or long-stored fruit, tends to suffer more from pectin release than does bittersweet fruit and will often give a very cloudy cider unless depectinized. Although there are some natural enzymes in both apple and yeast which will break down the pectin during fermentation, these enzymes are often rather weak and require some assistance.

You can buy a commercial pectic enzyme easily from any winemaking supplier. It must, however, be added at this point before fermentation, since these enzymes do not work efficiently in the presence of alcohol.

Vitamins and yeast nutrient

The next possible addition is that of vitamins and yeast nutrient. These may be bought labelled as such or may be added as thiamine (vitamin B1) and ammonium sulphate (or phosphate) respectively. The dosage rate is up to 0.2 milligrams per litre of thiamine and up to 300 milligrams per litre of ammonium salt (this is what was meant by 'amino nitrogen' in Chapter 2). The thiamine is needed by the yeast to complete the final step in turning sugar into alcohol, while the amino nitrogen is needed by the yeast to make protein and amino acids for its own growth. This is pretty much the same as human and animal nutrition – the yeast's carbohydrate or primary energy source is the apple sugar which is not in short supply, but the presence of other nutrients is vital for a healthy existence.

Apple juices are generally very low in yeast nutrients (unlike beer worts or grape musts) and so your fermentation rate will probably be much improved if you add these. The fermentation is also much less likely to 'stick' or to grind to a halt before completion; indeed it might be finished in two or three weeks rather than three months! The cider can therefore be racked and bottled sooner. On the other hand, it is undeniable that some of the finest ciders are fermented very slowly without the addition of nutrients, but the risks of things going wrong are correspondingly greater.

Traditional cider-makers used to hang a leg of mutton or a side of beef in the fermenting vat to boost the nutrient levels. The meat broke down slowly in the acid juice, releasing soluble amino nitrogen and vitamins which the yeast could use for growth. The supposed but largely apocryphal requirement of a few dead rats in every vat is a more colourful manifestation of the same idea.

It is possible to hedge your bets on this one and start off without nutrient. Then, if the fermentation grinds to a halt after a couple of months, you can add some thiamine to see if it will re-start. If this does not work, you can add some ammonium salt too. On the other hand, if you wanted a naturally sweet cider anyway, you can leave well alone and just be grateful. This though is a topic for Chapter 4.

SULPHUR DIOXIDE

The most important addition is that of sulphur dioxide, also known as Campden tablets, meta-bisulphite or SO_2. This material inflames great passions amongst some of the purist cider making lobby, who seem to regard it as dancing with the devil. However, it has a long and hon-ourable history, and the use of burning brim-stone (sulphur) as a sterilant in wine-making is supposed to date back as far as Homeric times in Ancient Greece. Certainly it was documented for cider making from the seventeenth century and the controlled addition of metabisulphite is far more accurate than the haphazard burning of sulphur candles in the barrels could ever be.

Historic use of SO_2 in cider making

'Lay brimstone on a rag, and by a wire let it down into the cider vessel, and there fire it: and when the vessel is full of the smoak the liquor speedily pour'd in, ferments the better!'

John Beale, writing in Evelyn's
Pomona of 1664

Dr Beale was brought up in Herefordshire but became vicar of Yeovil in Somerset. Along with John Evelyn, Beale was a tireless advocate of a scientific approach to cider making, and was a frequent correspondent on the topic to the newly formed Royal Society.

In simple terms what happens is that the sulphur dioxide (obtained from metabisulphite or burning sulphur) inhibits or kills most spoilage yeasts, moulds and bacteria, while permitting the most desirable fermenting yeasts (strains of *Saccharomyces cerevisiae*) to multiply and to dominate the conversion to alcohol.

Only small amounts of sulphur dioxide are used and its effectiveness depends quite critically on the pH of the juice. The table shows the appropriate levels to use for a normal cider fermentation. Cider juice, when pressed, con-tains large numbers of yeast, mould and bacteria which we do not want and only a very few of those that we do. The sulphite levels in the table have been empirically established based on lab-oratory investigations of the sensitivity of these cider micro-organisms and the likely amounts of natural 'sulphite binding' substances in the juice, in order to establish the dominance of benign fermenting yeasts and hence a much reduced chance of taints and off-flavours in the finished product. It is perhaps worth pointing out that the sulphite binding levels assumed in the table were those established in the 1970s for UK West Country cider apples harvested 'off the ground' and in typically variable condition. If you are using clean hand harvested fruit in other loca-tions you may have less sulphite binders in your juice and may be able to use less SO_2. Unfortu-nately there is no published data for this kind of fruit.

Sulphite is made naturally by many yeasts, even when not added, and it is a normal com-ponent of body chemistry resulting from the breakdown of sulphur-containing proteins and amino acids. Hence we all have enzymes inside us for handling and detoxifying sulphites. Any health concerns about sulphite derive from its excessive use at bottling, not during fermenta-tion, and from the fact that a very few people are hypersensitive to it in the free state. For that reason, where it has been added to alco-holic beverages, it is required to be labelled as a potential 'allergen' (which by strict immuno-logical definition it is not). However, it must be stressed that no sulphur dioxide remains free by the end of fermentation, since it becomes bound to various intermediate chemicals (prin-cipally acetaldehyde) which the yeast produces on its route from sugar to alcohol. The maximum amount of SO_2 which may be added to ciders

Sulphur Dioxide

ADDITION OF SULPHUR DIOXIDE			
Juice pH	SO$_2$ needed in parts per million (ppm)	ml of 5% SO$_2$ stock solution per litre[1]	Campden Tablets per gallon[2]
Above 3.8	Lower pH to 3.8 with addition of malic acid		
3.8	185	3.7	3
3.7	150	3.0	3
3.6	125	2.5	2
3.5	105	2.1	2
3.4	85	1.7	2
3.3	72	1.4	1
3.2	60	1.2	1
3.1	50	1.0	1
Below 3.0	None	None	None

Notes:

1 To make a 5 per cent stock solution of sulphur dioxide, dissolve around 10 grams of sodium or potassium metabisulphite in 100ml of water. (The metabisulphite salts contain around 50–60 per cent of available SO$_2$ depending on how they have been stored). Then 1ml of this per litre of juice (5ml per imperial gallon) gives around 50 ppm in the juice.

2 Campden tablets are formulated with metabisulphite, and yield around 50 ppm sulphur dioxide when each is dissolved in 1 Imperial gallon of liquid (or 60 ppm if dissolved in a US gallon).

by EU law is 200 ppm, hence the need to keep the juice pH below 3.8 if the added sulphite is to be effective.

YEASTS

This brings us to the final addition, that of yeast. Here there are fundamentally two routes: adding a defined cultured yeast or allowing a wild yeast fermentation to take place. The advantage of a cultured yeast (all of which are selected strains of *Saccharomyces cerevisiae*) is that it gets the fermentation off to a good start within hours, by providing a massive inoculum of healthy yeast cells which will multiply quickly and, with the assistance of the added sulphite, swamp out anything undesirable. The result will be predictable if a little one-dimensional, since only one type of yeast is involved. With a 'wild yeast' fermentation, results are less predictable since several yeasts will be involved, generally in a 'succession' with one following another.

However, the flavour may be more interesting and characteristic, though the fermentation will probably be slower.

Cultured yeasts

If you plan to use a cultured yeast, it is best to use a strain selected for white wine making. Do not use baking or brewing yeasts, which have been selected to have other properties which we do not require and which may even be unhelpful (for example, poor sulphite tolerance and poor flocculation ability at the end of fermentation). Many cider hobbyists in the US, who come from a brewing not a winemaking background, do recommend brewing yeasts but I am unconvinced by their arguments. Cider is a fruit wine not a beer, and beer-like flavours are not wanted by most cidermakers.

Some brewers also suggest that by using a 'low attenuation' brewing yeast they can preserve residual sugar in the cider after fermentation. This is not the case. The concept of 'yeast attenuation' has no place in wine or cider making. It refers to the ability of a brewer's yeast to digest complex malt sugars (maltotriose and higher oligomers) in beer wort towards the end of fermentation after the primary glucose and maltose are exhausted. These complex sugars do not occur in fruit juices. In cider all the natural sugars (sucrose, glucose and fructose) are fully fermentable by all normal fermenting yeasts, given sufficient nutrient.

In practice there is now a wide range of dried high quality wine yeasts available, which have been selected mostly by various research institutes from wine fermentations in France, Germany and the New World. They are then grown up, maintained and sold by commercial suppliers. (There are just a couple that claim to be have been selected from cider fermentations so far as I know, but I have seen no good provenance data for them, so it is difficult to be certain what they really are.) These yeasts are sold under many different brand names but in fact there are very few primary producers and many of the minor brands on the market are just re-packaged and re-named locally from bought-in bulk stock.

Some of the minor branded yeasts claim to confer specific flavours, such as 'Burgundy', 'Champagne' or to 'enhance varietal character-istics', but these claims should be taken with a pinch of salt and in any case are not relevant to cider making. For that reason it is a good idea to buy yeast which is branded by the primary producer and especially one who supplies data sheets which give the provenance and history of the yeast. Many of these can now be found on the internet.

Good supplier names to look out for are Lalvin (the wine retail arm of Lallemand, a Canadian company which is one of the world's biggest producers of yeast for all purposes), Erbslöh (German with UK agents), Siha/Begerow (another German company) and Maurivin (an Australian company). Other suppliers, notably in the US, include White Labs and Wyeast Labs.

Different selected strains of yeast can indeed

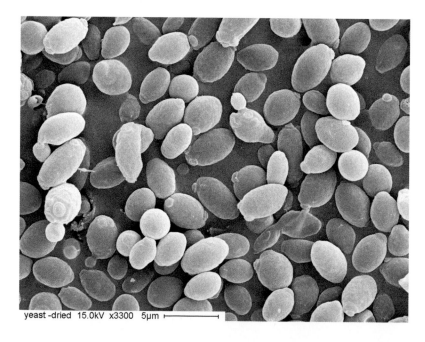

Electron micrograph of pure cultured yeast cells. Note the homogeneity of the cells.

yeast -dried 15.0kV x3300 5µm

produce detectably different flavours due for instance to a different balance of esters and higher alcohols. However, wine yeasts have not been specifically selected for cider fermentation and so the performance data available from wines must be interpreted with a good deal of latitude.

Key qualities for the craft cidermaker to look out for are probably cold tolerance and slow steady fermentation behaviour with low nutrient demand and low H_2S production. Ability to ferment to high alcohol levels is not important. For commercial 'chaptalized' cider production to high alcohol levels, which will later be diluted for sale, 'champagne' yeasts such as EC-1118 or Uvaferm BC (often also described as *Saccharomyces bayanus*) are often used. In my experience these can ferment out to give extremely dry and almost bitter single strength ciders with neutral aroma characteristics and I would tend to avoid them for craft use. Another yeast possibly worth avoiding is any whose provenance is given as Montrachet Davis 522, since this has a known tendency to produce hydrogen sulphide (H_2S – the rotten egg smell) at least in grapes. Some yeasts such as Lalvin 71B are known to metabolize and remove up to 20 per cent of the malic acid in apple juice as they ferment, which can be useful if your juice is quite acidic to begin with.

Amongst the wine yeasts which behave well and are regarded as contributing positively to craft ciders are those known as 71B-1122, V-1116, D47, DV10, QA23 and AWRI 350. (The latter, from the Australian Wine Research Institute, was used to make the Long Ashton commercial cider in the 1970s and 1980s when I was there).

As mentioned earlier most cider juices are deficient in nutrients, compared to grape musts which are in any case often fortified before fermentation. This means that the commercial wine yeasts are selected for a much richer nutri-

ent environment than a cider juice will provide and they may struggle to perform well in these circumstances. In particular, they may be more prone to produce off-flavours such as hydrogen sulphide when nutrients are lacking. It may be a wise precaution to add nutrients if you plan to use a cultured yeast, although there can be no hard and fast rules and some cultured yeasts are better able to stand low nutrient conditions than others. Yeast data sheets should give some guidance on this.

Method

Typically the yeast is grown up overnight as a concentrated 'starter' in juice or sugar solution following the manufacturer's directions and then pitched into the main bulk of juice the next day. Some of the more modern dried strains are simply re-hydrated for 20 minutes in plain warm water. If instructions are given, it is important to follow them, since manufacturers' technologies do differ.

If sulphur dioxide has been used, it is very important to wait overnight before adding the yeast culture. This is because the sulphur dioxide needs time to act against the wild organisms and it will also inhibit the added yeast too strongly if they are all added together. By standing overnight, the free sulphur dioxide largely disappears once its work is done, giving the added yeast a chance to get away without significant inhibition.

A loose bung or an airlock should be fitted after yeast addition, and fermentation should commence within two or three days if an active yeast culture is used.

Wild yeasts

Good quality cultured wine yeasts have been widely and commercially available for no more than fifty years. Before that, for many centuries, cidermakers relied on the wild microflora and many still do. A cider juice after pressing contains large numbers of yeast from the fruit and the orchard, many of the type known as 'apiculate' or lemon-shaped such as *Kloeckera apiculata* (also known as *Hanseniaspora valbyensis*). There may be up to 100,000 of them in every ml of juice. These yeasts will very quickly start a fermentation within hours, but they are not very alcohol tolerant (though they are tolerant of low temperature) and they soon die when the level rises to 2–4 per cent or so.

However, along with them there are a very few cells of wild *Saccharomyces cerevisiae*, which do not come in any significant numbers from the fruit but which survive from year to year on mills, press cloths, cider house walls and so on. These multiply in the juice while the *Kloeckera*

are working and so by the time the *Kloeckera* die out the *Saccharomyces* are ready to take over and finish the job of fermenting out all the sugar. Exactly the same is true in traditional winemaking too when a cultured yeast is not used. This 'succession' of micro-organisms means that many different flavours are produced so the cider becomes more complex.

Sulphiting

If no sulphite is used at all, the dominance of *Kloeckera* tends to mean that the final cider can be very high in ethyl acetate (which has an unpleasant solvent-like and vinegary aroma). However, *Kloeckera* are much more sensitive to sulphite than the *Saccharomyces* and so the levels of sulphite suggested in the table are intended to inhibit most of the *Kloeckera* but to allow most of the *Saccharomyces* to survive.

Wild yeast cells isolated from a cider fermentation. Note the diversity of forms; lemon-shaped 'apiculate' yeasts can be seen.

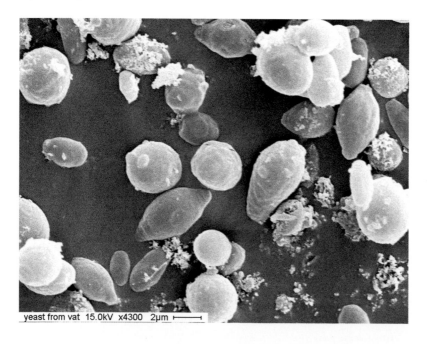

yeast from vat 15.0kV x4300 2µm

Hence a wild yeast fermentation which is sulphited will give cleaner flavours than one which is not. The old practice of burning a sulphur candle in the barrel shortly before adding the juice, as recommended by Dr Beale and others, achieved exactly the same thing although the levels were not well controlled.

The only drawback to the sulphiting is that because there are very few *Saccharomyces* cells in the first place, it takes much longer for them to grow up to the required level for the fermentation (10 million are needed per ml of juice from a starting population of maybe just a hundred or so). This process may take two or three weeks. However, if the juice is correctly sulphited for the pH and stays in a fermentation vessel fitted with an airlock, little harm will come to it while they grow. If after three weeks nothing has happened, it may be that there were simply too few cells to begin with and in that case you could 'cut your losses' and pitch a cultured yeast instead.

Although the sulphite addition table gives the 'standard' recommendations, based primarily on work at Long Ashton Research Station in the 1970s, it is possible to make the fermentation slightly more 'wild' by using only half the sulphite recommended. This will allow the development of rather more of the apiculate yeasts and hence slightly more diverse and interesting flavours; and this is what I do in my own cider making. If you omit the sulphite entirely, as some cidermakers do, you have no microbiological control at all and are therefore completely at the mercy of assorted unwanted mould and bacteria as well as apiculate yeasts. I prefer not to do that. However, if you are working with relatively acid dessert fruit (pH < 3.4), you may like to experiment with leaving out the sulphite, especially if you are adding a good cultured yeast, because adverse mould and bacteria find it hard to thrive in such conditions.

Advice for Beginners

For the beginner, I recommend:

- Using a pectolytic enzyme if dessert fruit is a major part of the blend;

- Getting yourself some pH papers and Campden tablets so you can add sulphur dioxide to the juice at the appropriate level;

- Adding a cultured wine yeast after standing the sulphited juice overnight (once you have some experience you can try wild yeast fermentations if you like);

- Monitoring the SG weekly;

- Keeping some nutrients on hand in case the fermentation begins to 'stick' or if you know that your fruit comes from big old trees with very low nutrient levels and you are not prepared to wait a few months.

FERMENTATION

As mentioned previously, a fermentation has a 'lag phase' which can last anything from two days to three weeks before there are any visible signs of gas production. Although it may appear that nothing is happening, in reality the yeast cells are quietly consuming sugar and multiplying to give a final level of around 10 million cells per single ml of juice.

Until enough cells have grown, and until the juice is saturated with the carbon dioxide which they produce, there is nothing much for anyone to see. But once this point is reached, there can sometimes be considerable frothing and evolution of gas which can make quite a mess. This can happen with any fermentation but is a particular feature of traditional wild yeast fermentations

An early frothy fermentation. (Photo: Ray Blockley)

A modern airlock pattern.

without SO_2, due to the rapid growth of *Kloeckera* yeasts early in the succession. Depending on the size and shape of your fermenting vessel, you may want to plug it loosely with cotton wool or with a lid left slightly loose or with an empty airlock, to keep insects and other undesirables away. At this stage it does not matter if some air gets into the fermenting juice. Indeed a small amount of air can be helpful for this initial stage of yeast growth.

When the initial frothing subsides, however, it may be worth topping up the vessel with more juice or a 10 per cent sugar solution to fill most of the headspace and at this stage you should fit a water-filled fermentation lock (airlock) to ensure that the flow of gas remains one-way. From now on, air should always be kept out. You can add a little red food dye to the water in your airlocks so that you can more easily see the bubbles. They will also need topping up from time to time as the water evaporates. Sometimes unwanted microbes or insects enter the airlocks, and I know one cidermaker who uses cheap

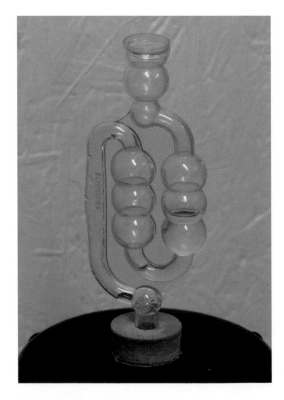

A traditional 'bubbler' airlock.

vodka in his airlocks as a sterilant for that reason. You can use a little 1 per cent sulphite solution too. The key idea is that if there should be any suckback from the airlock into the fermenting cider, due to day/night temperature variations for example, it should not introduce any adverse contamination.

Managing fermentation and racking

After a few days, the bubbling through the airlock should reassure you that fermentation is in progress. (If there are no bubbles, check that the airlock seal into the fermenter is gastight!). By weight, about half the sugar is lost by yeast activity during fermentation as carbon dioxide gas and the other half turns to alcohol. A tiny but very important fraction goes to make up the desirable flavour components which make cider or wine what it is.

The progress of the fermentation can be monitored every week or so by taking a sample and measuring with a hydrometer, and the fall in SG can be plotted on a graph against time (a fall of one degree SG per day is pretty reasonable). Depending on the design of your fermentation system, this may or may not be easy to achieve and it is better not to run the risk of contaminating the fermentation when taking a sample. A clean turkey baster can make it much easier to withdraw a sample, and one bought specially for the purpose can be an invaluable tool! Recording the SG figures makes it much easier to see whether sticking is occurring, and the nutrient and vitamin can be added then if necessary. Typically a cultured yeast fermentation with added nutrients kept indoors at a reasonable temperature may be complete in as little as a fortnight or so, whereas a wild yeast fermentation kept outdoors or in a barn may take up to three months and become almost imperceptibly slow in the depths of winter. Generally, for craft cider making, the slower the better.

As you follow the drop in SG with time, it will begin to level off and you should consider the first racking of the cider from its yeast at an SG of 1.005. Note that a fully fermented dry cider will have an SG less than 1.000, such as 0.996, since the SG of pure alcohol is 0.789 and once the sugar has gone the SG is determined by the proportions of alcohol and water, plus the natural malic acid and any natural non-fermentable materials such as sorbitol or glycerol.

By this stage most of the yeast should be well settled at the bottom of the fermentation vessel with only the occasional bubble of gas being produced. If the cider stops fermenting at an SG much higher than this, then it may be 'stuck', and nutrient addition together with twenty minutes vigorous aeration may help the yeast to grow again (the yeast does need some oxygen for growth but normally gets enough before fermentation begins).

It may also stop if the temperature falls too low, but this should need no attention from the cider maker. When the weather warms up again, the fermentation should re-commence. In fact, a cool fermentation (15°C or even below) is generally preferred for cider to retain the fruity flavours developed by the yeast, and there is no need to keep the fermentation especially warm. Above 20°C is not a good idea for craft cider. However, many cultured yeasts do struggle or stop if the temperature drops down to around 10°C and in that case it may be worth raising the temperature a little if you can. There is some evidence that wild yeasts continue to ferment more readily at low temperatures (down to around 4°C) than do cultured ones, although this may in part be down to a more diverse yeast population compared to a monoculture.

If the cider is rather acid at this stage, the first racking may be delayed for a month or two in the hopes of encouraging a wild 'malo-lactic fermentation' which is described later. In general, however, it is regarded as bad practice to leave a fully fermented cider on its yeast lees for more than a few weeks. I admit I have actually left ciders on their primary lees for up to a year on occasion, and without adverse effects, but this is not recommended. The danger is that the yeast may start to autolyze or break down to give unpleasant aromas in the cider if it sits on dead yeast for too long.

RACKING

The first racking should be into another clean vessel, trying to leave behind as much yeast as possible and with the minimum of aeration to the cider. This is generally done on a small scale with a clean plastic syphon tube fixed to a clean plastic rod so it rests just above the yeast deposit. You can buy purpose-designed 'racking tubes' which do this job.

It is up to you how you prime the siphon – ideally by pre-filling the tube with clean water rather than by sucking on one end. On a larger scale a suitable small pump may be used. Cheap 'drill pumps' for wine and cider are available. For more than 100 litres or so, a floor standing electric pump may be best and most such pumps are self-priming. Make sure it is one intended for use with cider or wine since it may soon corrode and introduce metal contamination into the cider if it is not.

With large pumps a clear plastic hose may be fitted to the outlet spigot of the tank (which should be above the yeast layer) and taken straight to the pump, rather than pumping out from the top of the tank. It helps to standardize on hoses and spigots which are of compatible diameters throughout, such as 15mm or 19mm, because then it is a simple job to push fit the hoses onto the spigots. A 'jubilee clip' (hose

A 19mm hose and push-fit connector.

Strengthened inlet hose (right) and regular outlet hose (left) on a small electric pump.

clamp) then ensures that the hoses do not fall off. The hose on the suction side of the pump should be of a reinforced design to prevent it collapsing inwards under vacuum.

The transferred cider should be run gently into the bottom of the new vessel without splashing – it is important to minimize the headspace and to prevent air contact as much as possible. This is partly to keep out any undesirable film yeasts or bacteria and partly to prevent 'chemical oxidation' which leads to flat dull flavours and a loss of freshness. This is why some people add 50 ppm of sulphur dioxide at every racking, although at the first racking this may be unnecessary if the cider is still in the last stages of fermentation. Sulphite added at this stage will almost certainly inhibit the malo-lactic fermentation, which may or may not be required (this will be discussed later).

A good deal of carbon dioxide remains in solution at the end of a cider or wine fermentation and to start with this is 'supersaturated' and well above its equilibrium saturation level of around 2g/L. Some authorities quote figures as high as 6g/L. This is an advantage as the cider is initially being handled since the CO_2 which is evolved will tend to prevent air from creeping back into the headspace. If you are using a pump to transfer freshly fermented cider you will almost certainly find it 'outgassing' with CO_2 bubbles liberated in the connecting tubing due to the mechanical agitation of the pump.

MATURATION

After the first racking the airlock is re-fitted until it is clear that gas evolution has ceased, when the vessel should be topped up with water or cider and tightly closed. A second crop of yeast will be thrown down as the cider stabilizes. The cider may remain in this state for several weeks or months, before a final racking to a closed container for bulk storage or directly into bottle. The airlock should be checked weekly and topped up if necessary, because no contact with air should be allowed at this stage.

MLF fermentation

Although in general the cider should not sit for long on a heavy crop of yeast, because the dead yeast will 'autolyze' which tends to give unpleasant flavours, a small amount of autolysis from the second crop may be helpful, because this releases nutrients which stimulate maturation through the so-called 'malo-lactic' fermentation (MLF).

MLF is sometimes erroneously called the 'secondary fermentation' but it has nothing to do with the true secondary yeast fermentation of beer. This causes much confusion to people with a brewing background and the term 'secondary fermentation' is best avoided if MLF is what is meant. The MLF is due to a specialized group of acid-tolerant bacteria (Lactobacillus or Oenococcus [previously known as Leuconostoc] species) which convert the malic acid of the apple to lactic acid, giving off more carbon dioxide in the process. Often, this happens in the spring when the weather warms up and the trees are flowering, giving rise to the old notion that somehow the trees and the cider are working in sympathy.

Sometimes the malo-lactic fermentation is to be welcomed since it lowers the total acidity and gives additional rounder smoother flavours, although in very low acid ciders it can reduce the acidity too far. In bittersweet ciders, depending on the bacteria involved, it may also produce characteristic 'spicy' or 'leathery' notes, sometimes described as 'old horse'. It may be recognized by the evolution of gas without renewed turbidity, whereas if a yeast re-ferments a sweet cider it becomes cloudy because the yeast cells are so large (typically 10 microns).

Malo-lactic fermentations, unless very heavy, tend to remain clear because the bacteria are so small (typically 0.5 microns). Some research during the 1990s also showed that these bacteria can live inside the pores of the old oak vats which are used in some factories for the maturation of cider. It is likely that it is these bacteria, rather than any direct extraction from the very old wood, which are responsible for the flavour changes and the 'rounding' that may take place as the cider ages in such vessels. Every season when a new batch of cider is added, the bacteria are just ready and waiting to start work.

The Malo-Lactic Fermentation

Malic acid is the principal acid in apple. It has two acidic carboxyl groups (COOH). One of these carboxyl groups can be removed by lactic acid bacteria to give CO_2 and lactic acid:

$$HOOC.CHOH.CH_2.COOH =$$
$$HOOC.CHOH.CH_3 + CO_2$$

Hence the acidity falls by 50 per cent and the cider becomes slightly carbonated as the carbon dioxide dissolves in the cider.

Malo-lactic fermentations are typical of some types of wine – for instance the 'buttery' notes of many Chardonnays are due to small amounts of diacetyl produced by MLF. In the past it was difficult to produce at will, but some good and reliable strains of lactic acid bacteria have now been selected and are available commercially for use in the wine industry and will be discussed further in Chapter 4. MLF may definitely be prevented by the additional use of sulphur dioxide at racking. Sometimes it reduces the acidity too far and sometimes the 'wrong' organisms take hold, producing other defects such as 'ropiness'

or worse 'mousiness' (which will be covered later). But if the original juice pH was no higher than 3.8 and the juice was properly sulphited to begin with, the chances are that MLF will be beneficial if it happens at all. Even if it does not, the cider will mature for several months as its flavour balance stabilizes and the harsher notes are smoothed out by slow chemical and biochemical reactions.

BOTTLING OR STORAGE

However, a simple dry cider does not generally profit by extended ageing, and by late spring or early summer the cider will be ready for bottling and drinking, or for a second racking into bulk store. When filling bottles or containers, do not pour cider into them, but fill them via a tube or siphon which extends all the way to the bottom of each vessel to prevent splashing and air pick-up. If you are bottling for commercial sale you should use a properly constructed filler system which can be calibrated to the correct fill volume. Simple manual systems consist of a small header tank and one or more spigots which reach right down into the bottles and shut off automatically once the target volume has been dispensed.

The golden rule at this stage is to minimize air contact whenever the cider is handled. It is a matter of preference whether you wish to add sulphur dioxide (about 50 ppm) to help with this. Many cidermakers add this level of SO_2 at bottling or storage both to inhibit oxidation and to provide protection against any unwanted microbial infection; after several weeks in bottle the level of free SO_2 drops quite considerably. To comply with EU law, you should not exceed a total addition of 200ppm SO_2 to any cider when all additions at fermentation and bottling are summed up.

Bottling

A dry cider with no added sugar and sufficient alcohol should be quite stable in clean, closed and well-filled glass bottles and should stand a minimal risk of any unwanted conversion to vinegar, though it may undergo MLF if not sulphited. If sealed with a screw or crown cap they can be stored upright, while if they are wine bottles sealed with a traditional cork they must of course be stored lying on their sides to prevent the cork drying out. Leave one inch of headspace in the bottles to allow for expansion in warmer weather.

Glass bottles normally used for cider in the UK are 500ml sealed with a crown cap or 750ml sealed with a 28mm threaded plastic cap. Both types can be re-usable and suitable caps can be purchased. Screw-cap wine bottles with an aluminium cap ('Stelvin' and similar) are not designed for re-use because the cap thread is moulded onto each individual bottle thread rather than being pre-threaded.

Plastic (PET) bottles are only useful for short-term storage of just a few weeks, because they can both gain oxygen and lose carbon dioxide quite quickly through their relatively thin walls, which blunts the flavour. Although it may seem counter-intuitive, oxygen can still diffuse into the bottle even if it is rigid with internal CO_2 pressure. By contrast, although few people realize it, bottling a still cider in glass can help to keep quite significant amounts of carbon dioxide gas in solution, not enough to show or be detected as bubbles but enough to positively benefit cider flavour and to prevent it from becoming 'dull'. The lower the temperature at bottling, the more CO_2 will remain in solution. Glass also prevents any oxygen diffusing in.

Bulk storage

For bulk storage, stainless steel winemaking tanks (preferably 316 grade) are ideal, if costly. But they are a capital investment which will

A variable capacity tank showing the lid in place.

A variable capacity tank with the lid supported to show the pneumatic tyre which forms the lid seal.

last almost indefinitely. Variable capacity tanks, which are sealed with a stainless lid fitted with a pneumatic tyre, can be obtained. The lid is suspended at the correct height to minimize headspace and the tyre is then inflated with a bicycle pump to hold the lid firmly in place against the walls of the tank. They are very convenient if you have fluctuating amounts of cider which may not completely fill a standard tank.

Thick-walled HDPE tanks as used for fermentation are not ideal for long-term storage for more than a few months, since oxygen will slowly diffuse inwards through the walls and lids. However, the presence of a thin layer of yeast can help to scavenge small quantities of oxygen by maintaining what biochemists describe as a 'reducing' environment. It is also wise to keep a low level of free SO_2 in bulk stored ciders, both for microbiological and oxidative control.

Professionally, a target value of 30ppm free SO_2 is usually recommended. This is monitored from time to time and topped up should the level drop below 20 ppm.

Draught

If you do not bottle, but dispense from draught, then split the cider into several smaller storage vessels as it is used, to minimize headspace and air contact. Cider should only be stored in tightly closed containers. It is possible to store and dispense dry cider from small casks or barrels but they should not be 'on tap' for more than a few days, or the cider will become progressively more oxidized as air enters the vessel each time a glass is drawn, unless you can replace the headspace air with CO_2 via some form of 'cask breather' system.

Bag in box

Modern 'Bag in box' systems use flexible laminated collapsible bags to keep the air away from the cider as it is dispensed and are an elegant solution to the problem. These were originally developed by the wine industry in Australia where they are known as 'wine casks'. They are widely available to small cidermakers and hobbyists in the UK, but not currently in North America. The product lifetime in such containers is generally reckoned as 3–6 months. On a small scale or for hobby use they can be filled manually with the bag supported on a stand, but automated and calibrated bag filling systems are also available for professional use. Air can slowly diffuse through the walls of

Bag in box, a modern dispense format for cider.

A home-made bag in box filler.

Cider and Air

The adverse effect of air on stored cider was no better described than by Ralph Austen in his *Treatise of Fruit Trees* published in 1657.

> 'In drawing the Cider, take heed of giving it too much Aire; if much Aire get in, it will very much deaden the Liquor. Too much Aire makes it flat and heartlesse and yet the cause (by many) is not perceived.'

Austen was a staunch Puritan and took an almost mystical view of fruit growing, seeing it as an allegory of human society, but he also managed a successful cider orchard and business in what is now the very centre of Oxford.

most plastic containers, however, and so glass or stainless steel are the best and the most impermeable barriers.

We have now looked at the steps in producing a still, dry cider which is the easiest sort to make. In the next chapter we shall look at variations of this process to produce other more complex types of cider.

4 CUSTOMIZING YOUR CIDER

The previous chapter considered the production of a straightforward dry, still cider. Although some people will enjoy what they have made, many first-time cidermakers who get to this stage find themselves deeply disappointed. The cider is often much dryer, more acid or more tannic and certainly much less sweet than they expect, and of course it has no bubbles. Although it is the 'real thing', it is a long way from what they have come to expect from the supermarket or pub. That is because a lot of modern 'soft drink' technology is used to produce the familiar market-leading brands even though they are alcoholic beverages.

In this chapter we shall look at how ciders can be modified to make them less challenging in flavour and how to produce sparkling and sweetened versions, concluding with an outline of 'keeving' – a traditional French and English technique which many regard as the pinnacle of the cidermaker's art.

MY CIDER IS NOT WHAT I EXPECTED

No apple flavour

Sometimes people complain that their cider does not taste of apples, though this is somewhat illogical since they do not generally expect a wine to taste of grapes nor a beer of barley. In fact very little of the original apple aroma comes through into a cider, except from a few highly aromatic apple varieties, since most of it is swept away during fermentation. Nearly all the initial cider aroma comes from new molecules generated by the action of the yeast, primarily from the sugars themselves which means that fundamentally all alcoholic beverages are very similar in their background flavour. Some of these molecules (especially some esters) are actually the same as those that were also originally present in the fruit.

However, the yeasts (and some benign bacteria) can also break down small amounts of what are known as 'flavour precursors' which are specific to the original fruit in question and which thereby give the drink its distinctiveness. In apple some of these are known. For instance, a glycosidic precursor which is virtually unique to apple liberates a component known as 1,3 octanediol, which then reacts with acetaldehyde formed during fermentation to give a dioxolane with distinctive 'cidery' characteristics that are not possessed by other drinks.

Likewise, a group of compounds known as hydroxycinnamic acids can break down under the influence of lactic acid bacteria to give volatile phenols such as ethyl phenol and ethyl catechol which contribute to the 'bittersweet aroma' of West Country ciders. It is quite probable that apple varieties differ in the range and type of precursors which they contain, hence conferring additional varietal characteristics. But it is fair to remark that apples when fermented into cider do not generally display the wide range of varietal characteristics that we are used to in grape wines, although some bittersharp apples such as Foxwhelp and Stoke Red do have distinctive estery characters which may persist after fermentation.

Blending

If you have made more than one cider in a season you may be planning to blend them. For instance, my own early season ciders are made from earlier cropping and more acidic fruit than those later on and they are deliberately blended after fermentation. Blending of ciders should always be carried out well before the final racking for storage or bottling. This is because the changes in acidity, nutrients and yeast levels, which occur when different batches are mixed, may affect the stability of the bulked cider and allow it to ferment further, even if the individual ciders were stable before blending. Similarly, if clear ciders are blended together they are quite likely to throw down a new haze or deposit which may need time to settle down. The general principle of blending is to ensure a flavour balance which is unobtrusive, particularly in terms of its acidity and tannin.

Sugar sweetened

If the cider is intended to be sugar-sweetened (which means it must be drunk within a fortnight, or pasteurized to prevent re-fermentation, as described later) it is best to take small test quantities of the ciders to be blended and sweeten these first to the SG which will be required for the final blend, for example, 1.020 for sweet, 1.015 for medium sweet, 1.010 for medium dry. This can be achieved by adding 40, 30 or 20 grams per litre of sugar respectively.

Acceptable tannin levels

Then a measuring cylinder should be used to blend equal parts of those ciders which are highest and lowest in tannin. The proportions should be varied until acceptable tannin levels are achieved and the operation repeated for any other ciders which are unbalanced in tannin composition. If the tannin levels are too low because no bittersweet fruit was used, it is possible to increase them by the addition of grape or other food grade tannin (in 0.1 per cent steps) until a satisfactory level is achieved, although the flavour from added tannin is rarely pleasing and often carries rather woody notes. Cold tea is sometimes used as a tannin source on a domestic scale. Careful note should of course be taken of the volumes used for blending and the amount of any tannin added. If the tannin levels are too high because of a large proportion of bittersweets, then fining with gelatin can be considered (as described in the next chapter).

Acidity

The trial blends which are now balanced for tannin can be blended for acidity following a similar routine. If the addition of acid is required, malic acid may be used in 0.1 per cent steps. Removal of acid is rather more difficult and is discussed in detail later. If the trial blends now have the correct tannin and acid balance, they can finally be corrected for other more subtle flavours and aromas by blending amongst each other.

Final blend

Finally, the main bulk of ciders can be blended according to the proportions determined by the trials but without the addition of the sugar at this stage. For reasons explained above, the ciders must be allowed to stabilize further in bulk store before correcting the sweetness. If a small amount of water is to be added to lower the alcohol content, it should be done at this time.

When blending, it is important to consider the temperature at which you expect the cider to be consumed. The sensory perception of sweetness, acidity, tannin and carbonation (see later) can be markedly temperature dependent. If you have blended at room temperature but your cider is drunk straight 'out of the fridge' it will be very different and may be somewhat disappointing. As a very rough rule of thumb, most dry still traditional ciders are probably best when drunk at room temperature, whereas sweetened and carbonated ciders can be blended to deliver their best flavour balance when chilled.

THE ACIDITY PROBLEM

If your cider has been made largely with dessert apples, it may be much more acidic than you like. The Eastern Counties or German style does not suit everyone's palate. Once the apple sugar is fermented away, it is surprising how stark the remaining acid becomes.

Approaches to the Problem of Acidity

• Blend with lower acid ciders until an acceptable balance is achieved;

• Sweeten the cider to offset the acid taste;

• Chemically neutralize the acid with calcium or potassium carbonate;

• Use a malo-lactic culture to reduce the malic acid level.

• For future fermentations, choose a yeast like 71B which can reduce the malic acid by up to 20 per cent.

Balancing acidity

If you have other batches of cider with lower acidity, you can simply blend until an acceptable balance is achieved. You may even try diluting the cider with water. You can sweeten the cider to mask or to offset the acid taste by the sweetening procedures given later. You can chemically neutralize the acid taste by the use of calcium or potassium carbonate in 0.1 per cent steps. Calcium carbonate tends to give a somewhat chalky taste due to the calcium ion, and potassium carbonate or potassium hydrogen carbonate is to be preferred. Even so, the maximum acceptable dose of potassium carbonate is around 0.3 per cent and this may be insufficient to do the job. Unfortunately the potassium remains in solution and affects the flavour; in addition it takes the potassium way outside normal cider levels so there may be legal implications if you plan to sell the cider.

Grape Acid Remedy is No Use in Cider

If you are used to removing acid in grape winemaking with Acidex or 'double salt precipitation', be warned that this dodge will not work in cider. Put simply, the reason is that malic acid is the chief acid in apples, whereas in grapes it is tartaric acid. Calcium or potassium malate remain soluble in cider while calcium or potassium tartrate are much less soluble in wine and can be removed by precipitation and racking. Not so in cider, unfortunately, so there is relatively little flexibility here.

MLF cultures

Until relatively recent times there were no other possibilities for the cidermaker. Although malo-lactic fermentation (MLF) will drop the acidity

A typical malo-lactic culture.

by half if all the malic acid transforms to lactic (see Chapter 3), the wild MLF organisms are highly unpredictable and in any case would not grow in an acidic cider, so this route is impracticable.

Now, however, MLF cultures are commercially available which will work down to pH 3.1 and in theory might convert a cider with as much as 1 per cent acid down to one with around 0.5 per cent. They do have a minimum temperature requirement of around 17°C though. I have myself taken a cider of 0.8 per cent acid down to around 0.5 per cent by this means over about two months in the moderate warmth of an English summer, using a commercial *Oenococcus oeni* culture (note that this organism was previously known by wine and cider makers as *Leuconstoc oenos*). In my view this opens up a whole new route to producing relatively balanced full juice ciders from dessert fruit, which

in the past would simply have been considered too acid by most consumers.

It is worth commenting that some cidermakers who have used MLF cultures, myself included, have noted how much less cidery and how much more vinuous the final product is. The lactic acid bacteria do far more in terms of flavour change than simply convert one acid to another – as described earlier, they may for instance generate characteristic 'buttery' notes.

One thing the cultures do not do, though, is to introduce the 'old horse' phenolic aromas which are regarded as characteristic of high quality bittersweet blends which have undergone wild MLF. The reason is that the cultures are generally strains of *Oenococcus* bacteria, which lack the enzymes needed to perform this phenolic change, whereas a wild MLF may also involve *Lactobacillus* and other species of lactic acid bacteria which carry a wider range of enzyme activities.

As with yeast, a single monoculture of MLF may not introduce the diversity of flavour which a mixed microflora may do. But, if acid reduction is the goal, the other flavour changes may still be an acceptable trade-off, and by using a culture you are unlikely to generate unwanted the bacterial 'off-flavours' which a wild MLF might produce.

DRY CARBONATED CIDER

I mentioned in Chapter 3 that even still ciders may well contain some dissolved carbon dioxide and indeed it improves the flavour greatly if they do. The saturation concentration of CO_2 in cider at 15°C is about 2 grams per litre (also expressed as '1 volume', meaning that one volume of gas is dissolved in the same volume of liquid). Below that it will improve the flavour, above

Acidity Testing during MLF

To get the best use from a MLF culture it is essential to know how fast the conversion is occurring and how much acid is being lost over time. This is best measured not in pH units but as total Titratable Acidity (see Chapter 3).

Acid titration kits

If you do not have access to a chemistry lab, acid titration kits for winemakers may be readily purchased from the normal suppliers. Once the culture is inoculated in the cider, the acid level should be measured weekly to see how fast it is dropping, the maximum theoretical loss being about 50 per cent of the original, as the dibasic malic acid is replaced by the monobasic lactic acid plus carbon dioxide. Obviously the cider should be tasted too, but the titration result will give a more accurate and quantifiable measure of acid loss with time. There may be no external signs and very few carbon dioxide bubbles to show that the culture is in fact working.

Convert to malic acid units

Winemakers' acid testing kits normally express the results in tartaric acid units – to convert to malic acid units the tartaric figure should be multiplied by 0.89. If expressed as sulphuric, multiply by 1.4. It is also possible to observe the change from malic to lactic acid visually by TLC ('thin layer chromatography') as many winemakers do – this is relatively simple for people with some laboratory experience who can get hold of the required materials. There are also TLC kits available from winemaking suppliers. Titration has the merit of providing a figure which can be recorded and correlated with the actual taste of the cider. Generally a cider which seems to be twice as acid by taste will have twice the acidity by titration too.

A hobbyist's acid testing kit.

MLF stopping early?

Measuring the acid level, in conjunction with TLC and tasting, gives some idea of where the cider is going and how close the MLF is to theoretical completion. The MLF might run out of steam if it runs out of nutrients or growth factors, for instance (which are poorly defined for MLF organisms, although some MLF nutrient cocktails are now on the market).

Reduction too great?

If the acid reduction seems to be too great, it might be possible to slow it down or stop it altogether by the addition of say 50 ppm of sulphur dioxide. An alternative possibility is the use of a winemaker's 'lysozyme' enzyme preparation, a relatively new technology which is sold to stop MLF occurring in low acid grape wines where it is not wanted. It is certainly possible to stop MLF by bottling and pasteurizing the cider as described later. If the goal is to produce a commercial bottled product in any case, this may be the most effective route.

that the cider will feel 'prickly' and at higher levels, noticeably effervescent. A cider which is undergoing MLF will be just on the threshold of detectable carbonation, but at best will be just slightly 'spritzig'. A typical carbonation level for a commercial cider might be 6 grams per litre ('3 volumes'). All levels above saturation will require a closed system to maintain the CO_2 in solution, which could be a screwcap, a wired cork, or a pressure keg.

It is quite possible to carbonate a cider artificially and indeed this is what is almost always done commercially, a technique known as 'force-carbonation'. The cider is cooled to increase the gas solubility, and CO_2 and cider are mixed dynamically in a specially designed pressure chamber before the product is bottled or kegged under counter pressure. Such systems are too expensive and complex for amateur use. On a single bottle scale this can be done in a Sodastream device, replacing water by cider in the bottles supplied (caution: this use is not covered by the manufacturer's warranty, and the cider tends to foam).

For those with a serious home brewing background, it can also be done in a pressure keg of the stainless steel 'Cornelius' type where the chilled cider is equilibrated slowly (over hours or days) with CO_2 from a cylinder and monitored with a pressure gauge to see how far the carbonation has proceeded. Polythene pressure vessels and caps and CO_2 cylinders of the 'King Keg' type are also available from home brew suppliers. These are best used for ciders which are already fully saturated with carbon dioxide and where the added CO_2 provides just a little 'top pressure'. Although moderately satisfactory I have found that the threaded brass inserts in the cap used for gas introduction and pressure relief are very prone to corrosion from cider since it is much more acidic than beer, and the metal parts tend to form green copper salts.

Bottle conditioning

It is more satisfying and elegant, however, to allow the cider itself to generate the carbon dioxide by 'bottle conditioning', and the secondary yeast activity also gives a more interesting flavour profile. The gas bubbles also tend to last for longer and are of smaller size and a finer 'mousse' than with forced carbonation.

One way of doing this is by racking and bottling the fermentation early, say at a gravity of 1.003 and allowing the cider to finish fermenting and to mature in the bottle. The CO_2 produced will dissolve in the cider to produce bubbles when the bottle is opened. One drawback to this technique is that it is often awkward to fill the bottles because of the active fermentation with gas bubbles everywhere, especially in the racking tubes where they block the flow. Also the yeast deposit in the bottle may be rather heavy and may be coarsely flavoured, so that it becomes difficult to pour the cider cleanly from the bottle for drinking.

A better plan is to rack the cider into bottles after fermentation to dryness, adding a small amount of priming sugar or syrup to each bottle (10g dry sugar per litre or a flat teaspoon per pint, which is roughly equivalent to 5 degrees of SG) and allowing the few yeast cells which are carried over to grow and to produce a true secondary fermentation of the added sugar to produce the gas. This can be very successful, although the bottom of each bottle will inevitably be a little cloudy when poured because there will always be some yeast deposit which will be roused up when the pressure is released. This problem can be lessened on a domestic scale by storing the conditioned cider in a pressurized keg or barrel similar to those used for home-made beer (as described earlier). If the yeast has totally died out by the time you bottle (unlikely but possible) you may have to add a *very* small amount of dried fermenting yeast to the bulk cider (1–2 grams per 100 litres).

Traditional method: Champagne bottles

The ultimate way of avoiding the yeast problem is to produce a sparkling cider by the *méthode traditionelle* which is used in the production of champagne and other such sparkling wines. In brief, a fully fermented dry base cider is bottled in champagne bottles together with a charge of sugar syrup and an inoculum of champagne yeast or special encapsulated yeast. The bottles are sealed with special over-sized crown caps (29mm) and allowed to ferment on their sides for at least a year. During this time the yeast slowly carbonates the product, following which it dies and 'autolyses' thus producing new flavour components. (These flavours are likely to be more desirable than the coarse flavours produced by autolysis of a large crop of primary fermenting yeast).

The bottles are then inverted and turned every so often ('riddling') for several weeks until all the yeast is collected in the neck. This is then frozen in an ice-salt mixture, the bottle is opened, the frozen yeast plug is forced out by gas pressure, and the bottle is topped up with a small amount of sugar syrup (the *dosage*) for sweetening. It is then resealed with a cork and wire cage before the majority of the gas can escape. The *dosage* should not re-ferment if all the yeast has been cleanly removed, and the very high pressure (6 bar) tends to inhibit yeast growth.

That is the principle, but the individual practices vary and are a 'trade secret' from producer to producer. Some automation is possible; for instance a machine known as the 'gyropallet' can replace the hand riddling stage, and specially designed freezing units can replace the traditional ice-salt mixture. There are now a few such craft ciders available on the UK market which can command the high prices required to offset the labour-intensive production method.

Strong glass bottles

Any bottles used for carbonated ciders must be designed to withstand the pressure generated by the gas or there is a serious risk of them bursting and causing injury (not to mention the mess!). Heavyweight (approximately 500g per 500ml bottle) multi-trip glass beer bottles which are sealed with a crown cork should be available from home-brewing suppliers. More robust still are proper champagne bottles (approximately 900g per 750ml bottle) which can be sealed with the correct mushroom cork or its plastic equivalent. Either way a wire cage must be used to prevent the stopper popping out under pressure. Threaded 28mm screwcap glass bottles must never be used for bottle-conditioned ciders since they are not intended to stand the pressure.

From the historical point of view, it is now fairly well established that the first heavyweight glass bottles for beverage use were produced and used specifically for storing naturally sparkling cider in the Forest of Dean (Gloucestershire), due to the local availability of coal which enabled higher temperatures and stronger product to be achieved in the glass furnaces. This was happening by the 1650s and pre-dates the French 'invention' of champagne by some fifty years at least. It is fairly clear that the principles and practice of successful bottle fermentation were borrowed by the French from the English and not the other way about!

The table shows the relationship between the amount of residual sugar and the gas pressure produced if it all ferments out. For comparison, a regular car tyre is pressurized to only about 30 psi (pounds per square inch) or 2 bar (atmospheres) in metric units.

There is evidence that yeast growth itself is inhibited by the high CO_2 pressures found inside a champagne bottle at around 90 psi (6 atmospheres), so that if more sugar than 20g/l is

Residual sugar and gas pressure				
Unfermented sugar content		**CO_2 present if all sugar ferments out**		
SG	**Grams per litre**	**Grams per litre**	**Bottle pressure at 20°C (psi/ bar)**	**Safe bottle type**
0.998	Nil	2 *(saturation)*	Nil	Any
1.003	10g/l	7	45/3	Strong crown cap
1.008	20g/l	12	90/6	Strong champagne

present, it may not all be fermented. However, it is not possible for the amateur to guarantee this and it is wise to err on the side of caution. The figure of 20g/l of sugar should not be exceeded.

PET bottles

For mainstream force-carbonated product at the lower end of the market, the industry has now gone over almost entirely to PET (polyethylene-terephthalate) bottles which are lightweight and hold a moderate pressure well. Also, if they do burst, there is less risk of injury since there is no flying glass. If you are making a small amount of cider for home use, you can recover, rinse and re-use these bottles for naturally conditioned cider several times if they have previously contained other carbonated drinks. If you cannot scrounge sufficient secondhand bottles or you are working on a larger scale, you may have to buy new PET bottles from a specialist supplier. Large bottlers blow their own on site to reduce transport costs.

However, the walls of PET bottles are gas permeable so they will lose their carbonation over time as CO_2 escapes, and at the same time oxygen will diffuse in. Hence they are not recommended for storage over more than a few months. Although it may seem counter-intuitive, it is a fact that a PET bottle which is rigid due to

internal CO_2 pressure does not prevent oxygen from diffusing back in at the same time (this is due to the physics of 'partial pressures' of gases). This process leads to a more rapid maturation, more secondary yeast growth and eventual quality loss in the cider.

The storage life of bottle-conditioned ciders in glass may be reckoned as several years. Indeed, there is subjective evidence that the cider improves after the first year or so as the small amount of remaining yeast autolyses and produces more complex flavours. Many craft cidermakers will tell you that they believe their naturally conditioned ciders are at their best in their second and third year. After that a decline sets in so that the ciders, though still drinkable, become progressively less interesting and more one-dimensional in flavour.

Cask conditioned cider

Unlike beer, cask conditioning of cider does not follow naturally from the production process. Beer is made from malted (part-germinated) barley in which starch is broken down to give a range of simple sugars like glucose and more complex ones like maltose, maltotriose, malto-tetrose and so on. It is the slow and difficult secondary fermentation of these complex sugars after the glucose is gone which allows for the creation of cask-conditioned 'real ale'.

By contrast, cider is a fruit wine and all its sugars are simple and fully fermentable to dryness (given sufficient nutrient). Cider and wine cannot therefore be made to undergo a true cask conditioning and there is therefore no 'real ale' equivalent in the cider world, despite what some people wish to believe. Since craft cider, unlike beer, can only be made at one time of year this further limits the possibilities of catching the product just at the critical moment.

However, it is possible to use the bottling techniques described earlier to produce a cider which is allowed to undergo a secondary yeast fermentation in a cask. This is done by taking a fully fermented dry cider and adding to it some yeast and a little priming sugar just as described for a dry bottle-conditioned cider. Once the renewed fermentation is under way, the cider may be treated as if 'cask conditioned' and consumed while in that state. This is not ideal since the first glasses drawn will be sweet and barely sparkling, while those drawn a week later will be drier, cloudy and much fizzier. A week after that and the cider may be flat again. A pressure keg will help to mitigate some of these problems by retaining the gas and slowing the fermentation to an extent, but essentially you are trying to force cider into a consumption format for which it is not well suited.

SWEETENED CIDERS

Even a 'dry' cider will have a little residual sweetness both from the small amounts of non-fermentable sugars such as xylose and sorbitol which exist in the original juice and from glycerol produced during fermentation. In addition, the perception of sweetness is considerably influenced by factors other than simple sugar level. For instance, the more acid there is in a cider, or the colder it is served, the less sweet it will appear. Traditional dry ciders are best drunk at room temperature rather than from a refrigerator. The serving context is also important. A cider to be drunk with a meal can tolerate more acidity and less sweetness than a cider drunk on its own.

Commercial solutions

However, there is an undeniable demand for ciders which are medium dry (SG about 1.010) or medium sweet (SG about 1.015) and so some way often has to be found of adding or retaining sugar without running the risk of it re-fermenting. This is difficult if any yeast remains in the presence of an adequate supply of nutrients because it will immediately get to work on the added sugar. Typically, a sugar-sweetened cider has a life of no more than two weeks before it starts to re-ferment.

Commercially, the problem is nowadays tackled by centrifugation and filtration of dry cider to remove most of the yeast, followed by addition of sugar syrup and cold sterile filtration through 0.2 micron membranes and final bottling in 'aseptic' clean-room conditions. Such a process makes stringent microbiological demands that are not achievable on a domestic scale.

Pasteurization to kill the yeast is a more traditional commercial technology, where the sweetened cider travels through flow-through heat exchangers operating, for example, at 90°C with a residence time of 30 seconds before hot filling, or by a more traditional 'tunnel' pasteurizer in which pre-filled bottles pass on a belt through sprays of hot water followed by a cooling zone. Such equipment is generally beyond the budget of the hobbyist or small producer.

Batch pasteurization

However, it is quite possible to batch pasteurize bottled sugar-sweetened cider on a small scale in tanks of hot water, and although a slightly cooked note may be generated it is often worth the trade-off. The cooked note can be minimized by adding 30–50 ppm SO_2 to the cider before bottling and by not overheating. A water bath of some sort and a digital kitchen thermometer is required for this. The water bath can range from a large pan on a stove-top up to purpose built electrically heated units holding anywhere between a dozen and a hundred bottles. It is a benefit if the bath contains a false bottom to prevent bumping and can be arranged with some form of rack or crate to lift the bottles in and out of the bath.

Bottled

Uncapped bottles of sweetened cider with a 1-inch headspace are stood in the bath and heated until the temperature of the contents reaches 66°C; the bottles are capped, removed and then laid to cool on their sides to sterilize the inside of the necks and caps.

An alternative procedure is to fill and cap the bottles and completely cover them in the water bath (maybe by lying them stacked on their sides), then bring the temperature up to 66°C and hold it there for twenty minutes so that the internal temperature of the bottles reaches the set temperature. Obviously this procedure may result in bursting bottles since they are already sealed, so safety goggles should be worn. In this case a larger headspace (1½–2in) in the bottles will reduce the risk. When sweetening cider in bulk before bottling, it is usually more conveni-ent to make up the calculated sugar into a 50 per cent syrup with a portion of the cider and then stir this into the container, rather than trying to dissolve dry sugar into the entire bulk.

The time and temperature conditions required for pasteurization are sometimes expressed in pasteurization units or PUs. Up to a point, a long pasteurization time at a lower temperature can be equivalent to a short time at a higher temperature, but the relationship is not linear and the PU concept takes account of that math-ematically. Typically, 50 PUs are recommended for a sweetened bottled cider to achieve a stable finished product, and the conditions outlined previously will in practice give 50 PUs. However, the theory and calculation that lies behind PUs is somewhat complex and will not be discussed further in this book.

Bag-in-box

With care, it is also possible to pasteurize sweet-ened cider for 'bag-in-box' dispense. The bag supplier's recommendations should be fol-lowed for this but, in general, the same prin-ciple applies as for pasteurizing in bottle. Each open but filled bag should be supported and immersed in the pasteurizer as deeply as pos-sible, with the cap loosely fitted, so that the con-tents reach 66°C, when the cap is firmly sealed before inverting the contents. It is also possible to fill and pre-seal the bags and pasteurize them totally immersed as for bottles, though the bags may 'balloon' alarmingly due to the release of dissolved CO_2. As I understand it the bags are only rated for a temperature of 55°C but they can withstand higher temperatures for a shorter time. Some larger cider makers 'hot-fill' the bags with pre-warmed cider, which is the equivalent of pasteurization but requires more complex controlled equipment such as a flow-through heat exchanger to be effective.

Back sweetening with juice

It is possible to use apple juice as a sugar substi-tute for 'back sweetening' of ciders. Obviously this increases the total volume and dilutes the alcohol somewhat since you may need 10–20 per cent of juice added to get the required sweetness, but it may make for a more interesting flavour profile and it may also be beneficial in diluting the final alcohol content. Logistically, fresh apple juice is not normally available in spring or summer when cider bottling is likely to be carried out, so if you plan this route you may need to deep-freeze some juice in advance. Effective pasteurization is very important in this case since the juice itself is likely to have far more yeast associated with it than dry sugar or a 50 per cent sugar syrup.

Using preservatives and artificial sweeteners

If you want to sweeten dry ciders with added sugar but you do not want to pasteurize them or to consume them within a week or two, it is important that they should be racked and stored for several months after fermentation is complete, to allow the yeast to die out completely before the sugar is added. Otherwise the risk of re-fermentation is considerable.

Preservatives to retard fermentation

The chances of re-fermentation can be reduced by the addition of yeast inhibitors such as potassium sorbate or benzoate at levels up to 200 ppm in the EU (400 ppm in the US). Benzoate addition is not permitted in the EU if the cider is to be sold. Sorbate is most effective if combined with say 50 ppm of SO_2 added at the same time because it increases the 'hurdle' effect against micro-organisms and inhibits malo-lactic bacteria which may otherwise attack the sorbate to give a 'geranium-like' off-flavour. However, no preservative has

the power to stop fermentation completely while any significant numbers of viable yeast cells remain, and some spoilage yeasts such as *Zygosaccharomyces baillii* are totally preservative resistant. At best, preservatives are a way of retarding the almost inevitable re-fermentation which will take place, and cannot be recommended as a trustworthy alternative to pasteurization.

Artificial sweeteners

An alternative route is to use artificial, non-nutritive, or intense sweeteners which will not re-ferment. These are sweeteners other than sugar and include saccharin, acesulfame-K, and sucralose. Aspartame, used in some soft drinks with a short shelf-life, breaks down in acid solution and is not stable enough for use in cider. Stevia extracts (such as Rebaudioside A) are not currently permitted for cider in the EU but have been used by some amateurs. Most of these have flavour drawbacks – for example saccharin has a bitter aftertaste and stevia has a clinging sweet aftertaste. Sucralose (sold retail in diluted form as Splenda) is the best of the bunch and is permitted for cider in the EU up to 50mg/litre (around 20–30 mg/litre is a typical dose). Small compressed tablets of Splenda are each equivalent to one teaspoon of sugar in terms of sweetening power, so are ideal for just one glass of cider at a time. However, like all artificial sweeteners, sucralose lacks 'body' or 'mouthfeel' compared to sugar, as a like-for-like comparison in cider will soon show. But because its taste profile is superior to saccharin and it does not 'linger', sucralose can also be used with some success to sweeten dry carbonated or bottle conditioned ciders, thus obviating the need for pasteurization. If cider is for sale in the EU and the UK the presence of any artificial sweetener such as saccharin or sucralose must be indicated on the label.

But is it really craft cider?

The use of preservatives and artificial sweeteners, though perfectly safe, seems to me to be one step removed from the craft ethos. I prefer to use sugar and pasteurization, which seem to me to be more 'natural' interventions. Saccharin has been used by UK 'farmhouse' cidermakers for 120 years since its commercial introduction in the 1890s, and indeed for so long that many such producers now mistakenly regard it as both natural and traditional since even their great-grandfathers were using it!

Prior to those days it required genuine skill to make and maintain a naturally sweet cider, as described later in this chapter. The introduction of saccharin changed all that. If you go to a rural cider farm or a cider festival in the UK nowadays and are offered a choice of sweet, medium or dry ciders from the barrel, you can be almost certain that an artificial sweetener such as saccharin (or possibly sucralose) is responsible. But their use is not especially publicized, nor are they generally labelled as the law requires. Saccharin is also widely used as a partial sugar replacer in commercial bottled ciders, as it is in many soft drinks, but there it is properly labelled.

Amongst the natural low intensity sweeteners, lactose or milk sugar is effectively unfermentable and is sometimes recommended by hobbyists for sweetening cider, but its sweetening power is about half that of regular cane or beet sugar (sucrose) so it becomes an expensive proposition. It also has an odd mouthfeel at the levels required and might also be attacked by lactic acid bacteria. Xylitol is a non-fermentable sugar alcohol used mostly in sugar-free confectionery. It has about the same sweetness as sugar, although much more expensive, and is occasionally used by hobbyists to sweeten ciders. The related compound sorbitol occurs naturally in apples and pears, is also non-fermentable, and is a minor component of all ciders. It is not a practicable sweetener due to its laxative effect. Fructose (so-called fruit sugar) is about one and a half times sweeter than sucrose, so less is needed, but since it is fully fermentable by most yeasts its use cannot be recommended.

SWEET CARBONATED CIDERS

One possible approach to the conundrum of making a sweet but sparkling bottled cider on a small scale without pasteurization is to combine the use of non-fermentable sucralose to provide sweetness with that of bottle conditioning to provide carbonation. Both techniques have been described earlier. This is typically a hobbyist's solution but is also used by a few small commercial producers in the UK. It is safe and low-tech, and requires no specialist equipment.

Using sugar for carbonation and sweetness

An alternative is to use sugar to provide both the carbonation and the sweetness, by allowing a partial re-fermentation to take place in the bottle but to stop it by pasteurization once the required level of carbonation is reached. I have never carried this out myself but it is described in a booklet from 1976 published by the Canada Department of Agriculture as follows:

Before bottling, add 1–3oz (28–85g) of sugar to each gallon (4.5 litres) – 3oz gives a sweet cider. Fill the bottles leaving 1–1½in (2.5–3.8cm) of headspace, cap them and hold at 70°F (21°C) to allow bottle fermentation to take place. The carbon dioxide produced gives the cider sparkle or head. Open a trial bottle each day, and if enough carbonation has developed, the cider is ready to be pasteurized. Place the bottles upright on the bottom rack of a canner or double boiler and cover the bottles completely with water. Fill one uncapped bottle with water and raise it from the bottom so that the neck is above the water level. Put a thermometer into a cork so that the bulb is at the centre of the bottle when the cork is in place resting on the neck of the bottle. Heat the water until the thermometer in the test bottle registers a temperature of 150°F (66°C); pasteurization is then complete. Remove the bottles from the water and place them on their sides on several layers of newspaper. After 2 or 3 minutes place the bottles in warm water and leave them at room temperature until the cider is cool.

I suggest goggles and strong gloves for this and a rehearsed procedure for dealing with broken glass since burst bottles are a very real possibility. It is worth noting that a cider which is carbonated to 2 volumes of CO_2 has an internal pressure at 20°C of around 1.3 atmospheres or 20 psi. But the same bottle at 66°C has an internal pressure of nearly 6 atmospheres or 90 psi. Such pressures are sustainable for a short time only, even if good quality crown-cap bottles are used, and appropriate precautions must be taken.

Most amateurs do not attempt to measure the carbonation levels of their ciders. However, this is possible by using a pressure gauge known as an aphrometer and a set of temperature conversion tables. The gauge is equipped with a needle that penetrates the bottle cap. The initial CO_2/air mixture is vented off and the true CO_2 pressure is then measured after re-equilibration. By means of the tables, this can be converted to a 'volume CO_2' measurement. The test is destructive and is therefore only used on one or two samples in a batch.

Contract bottling

The business-oriented craft cidermaker who wants to sell a carbonated sweetened product to

Cider on its way to the contract bottler.

Cider returned from the contract bottler.

rival those on the supermarket shelf, but of superior quality due to its provenance and full juice content, would be well-advised to consider contract bottling. At the time of writing, there are two companies offering this facility in the English West Midlands and they are used extensively by medium-scale craft cidermakers who sell through farmers' markets and local stores. Partial or full service is offered to include sugar sweetening to a required SG, filtration, carbonation, bottling, pasteurization and labelling.

Although all the required equipment to do the job can be purchased, it is expensive, needs skilled maintenance and will be lying idle for much of its life, so it may make much more economic sense to contract this operation to a professional bottler. The likely minimum quantity handled will be 200–1,000 litres. Even as a hobbyist, I have had batches of my own cider bottled this way very satisfactorily, not specifically for sale but simply for my own private use by family and friends. It is quite a comforting thought to have several hundred bottles of cider safely stored away which I know will remain drinkable for several years – though it comes at a cost, it is true!

TRADITIONAL SWEET CIDERS

Traditionally, naturally sweet ciders were made from slow fermentations which were poor in nutrients. Such fermentations were not uncommon in the days when most cider fruit came from big old trees with low nutrient status. Those orchards were never fertilized and often had livestock running in them during the summer. As the animals grew they absorbed the nutrients from the grass and took them when they left, leaving none for the trees.

Modern fruit from dedicated bush orchards has much higher nutrient status and so is generally unsuitable for making naturally sweet ciders. It is also worth noting that most 'vintage' cider apple varieties take up less nitrogen from the soil in any case, and therefore can be inherently slow fermenters if grown in orchards which have very little fertilizer input. So if you have an old orchard of your own, or your orchard is low in nutrients because of the trees you grow and the way you manage it, then you may be able to make naturally sweet ciders in the old way. This is also more likely to be successful if you use wild yeast fermentation rather than adding a vigorous cultured yeast. Juices which are fermenting inherently slowly and which show an SG loss of less than one degree per day are suitable for this treatment.

How to make it

The cider is racked initially into a new clean tank when it reaches SG 1.020, leaving most of the yeast behind. The airlock is re-fitted. The continued fermentation will then become even slower and the sweet cider is racked again (and preferably filtered) at SG 1.015–1.012 for a medium sweet cider. After this racking it is worth waiting several weeks (under an airlock) to ensure that no further fermentation takes place, before sealing the vat or bottling off. Where bottles are used, they should preferably be of the champagne type in case any re-fermentation does take place. If all that sugar were to re-ferment you would be over the safe limit for a 'bottle bomb'.

The factors that generally limit yeast growth are the lack of nutrients and the build-up of CO_2 in a closed bottle (since excess CO_2, although produced by the yeast, is also toxic to it to a certain extent). It is wise to make a test bottling after the second racking and lay the bottle down in a closed box for three weeks in a warm place (25°C). Then, wearing gloves and goggles, open the bottle and assess the level of carbonation. If it is obviously excessive, leave the bulk for a fortnight longer and re-test before doing the final bottling. If the carbonation is nil to slight, it will be safe to bottle the bulk. Either way, the bottles should be stored cool and in a place where they would cause no damage or injury should the worst happen. A carbonated drink at 30°C contains up to twice the internal pressure of one at 15°C as the gas is driven out of solution by the heat.

It is best to choose days on which the temperature is low and the barometric pressure is high for the racking and bottling operations, since this will help to keep suspended yeast to a minimum and will retain the maximum amount of dissolved carbon dioxide in the cider. The success of the whole process depends on reducing both yeast and nutrient levels to a minimum so that re-fermentation of the remaining sugar is unlikely to take place. Sweet ciders of this sort may have a slight 'prickle' to them, particularly in bottle, since a very slow fermentation may continue to generate carbon dioxide until the increased CO_2 level itself intoxicates the remaining already stressed yeast.

Naturally sweet

The procedure described is ideal for single-variety demonstration ciders or for those which need no further blending – the flavour tends to be 'fruitier' since the sweetness is derived from unfermented juice rather than from added sugar. The alcohol level in the cider is of course less than if it had been fermented to dryness because only a part of the sugar has been converted.

It is abundantly clear from descriptions in the literature that many (perhaps most) bottled ciders were made in this way for several hundred years until the early twentieth century, and even as late as the 1960s in some cases, and were naturally sweet and sometimes slightly sparkling to some degree. These have almost entirely disappeared from memory in a couple of generations, in part due to the 'law of unintended consequences' following changes in apple orcharding practice and hence higher nutrient levels in the juice and cider. In addition, perceived customer demand for a totally consistent retail product led the large cider producers to embrace added sweetening, forced carbonation and pasteurization techniques from the early years of the twentieth century onwards.

KEEVING – A FRENCH AND ENGLISH TRADITION

The ultimate style of naturally sweet sparkling cider is made by a method known as 'keeving'. This is traditional both in western England and the northwest of France, but whereas it has virtually died out as a commercial proposition in this country, it is still very much alive for the production of *cidre bouché* in France. The underlying principle is to remove nutrients from the juice by complexation with pectin at an early stage to ensure a long slow fermentation which finishes and can be bottled while still sweet but with little fear of any re-fermentation later.

Traditional process

The traditional process begins with a blend of late season fully ripened mostly bittersweet fruit, taken from mature orchards which are naturally low in nutrients but fairly high in tannin. Dessert fruit is much less likely to be successful here, due to its generally low tannin and high nutrient

levels. The sugar level should be at least 12 per cent (SG 1.055). The fruit is stored until a cold day late in the year when the temperature is about 5°C and expected to remain so for a week or more. The fruit is washed and milled in the normal way, but the pulp is then packed into barrels to stand for up to twenty-four hours. This is the procedure of *maceration* or *cuvage*, terms with no particular English equivalent. During this time, oxidation slowly proceeds which develops some juice colour, but more especially pectin leaches out of the apple cell walls into the juice. The juice is then pressed out, rich in colour and thick in texture and is run into clean barrels (previously sulphited by burning 10g of 'sulphurated string' inside them). No yeast is added.

Since the temperature is low, no significant yeast fermentation takes place in the first few days, but the natural pectin esterase enzymes in the apple juice slowly change the pectin to pectic acid. This forms a gel as it cross-links with the natural calcium in the juice and a 'brown cap' (the *chapeau brun*) rises slowly to the surface as it picks up gas bubbles from the early stages of a very slow fermentation conducted by yeasts trapped in the gel. In seventeenth century English writings, this cap was picturesquely known as the 'flying lees'. Some of the pectin also combines with juice protein and tannin and falls as a sediment to the bottom, leaving a clear juice between the two. In French this process is known as *défécation*. If excessive yeast growth begins too soon, the *chapeau brun* is replaced by the normal *chapeau blanc* and turbulent fermentation takes over. In this case keeving has failed and the fermentation is allowed to proceed in the normal way. With some varieties of apples, no head forms at all and so they cannot be keeved.

If the keeving has been successful, however, the clear juice between the top cap and the bottom sediment is very carefully pumped or syphoned

into another pre-sulphited fermentation vat. It is now allowed to ferment under an airlock in the normal way (with its own yeast), but this fermentation will be very slow because most of the nutrients in the juice will have been left behind in the cap and in the sediment. Because the pectin is negatively charged, and the nutrients such as thiamine and asparagine (the major amino acid in apple) are positively charged, the nutrients are attracted to the pectin gel and hence removed from the system. Scientific studies have shown that the pectin and the amino nitrogen nutrients are reduced by at least 50 per cent during keeving. The number of yeast cells is also substantially lowered by entrapment. With the slow resulting fermentation it should be no problem to make a naturally sweet cider by racking initially at an intermediate SG and proceeding as described earlier. Eventually the ciders are bottled on a cool high-pressure day and slowly continue to develop 'condition' in the bottle.

A specimen keeve in a glass jar.

The top of a *chapeau brun* in progress.

Natural but tricky

The advantage of keeving is that it can produce a naturally sweet and well-coloured cider, brilliantly clear due to the removal of pectin and full of flavour because of the low nutrient levels during fermentation. The disadvantage is that a lot of it depends on luck – the correct fruit, cold weather, benevolent strains of wild yeast and freedom from bacterial infections. However, it has been made much more controllable in recent years by some key items of technology. On a commercial scale in France, for instance, the vats are refrigerated at 4°C, the *chapeau* is encouraged to rise by bubbling nitrogen gas through the system and centrifugation is used to remove excess yeast if the fermentation should develop too quickly. These technologies are not available to the amateur or small producer, but there are two important parts of the system which are – calcium and pectin methyl esterase (PME) enzyme.

Calcium chloride

Calcium is required to form the pectate gel. Depending on where the apples are grown, there may or may not be sufficient calcium naturally present in the juice, but it can be added in the form of a calcium salt and this makes the keeve much more reliable and gives a thicker denser cap. In the past a mixture of calcium carbonate (chalk) and common salt (sodium chloride) was used, the chloride helping to moderate yeast growth. Nowadays it is possible to buy food-grade calcium chloride which can be added instead and does the same job more conveniently (and without raising sodium levels!). The maximum dosage used is 400 parts per million or 4 grams per 10 litres, which is stirred into the juice after pressing. Food grade calcium chloride is usually supplied as the dihydrate ($CaCl_2.2H_2O$) or as the hexahydrate

($CaCl_2.6H_2O$), so allowance must be made for the 'water of crystallization'. In practice this means adding up to 5.3 grams of the dihydrate or 8 grams of the hexahydrate to every 10 litres of juice. It is best to make up the calcium chloride as a concentrated solution in water or juice before adding it to the bulk so it can be well dispersed by stirring.

PME enzyme

The PME is required to de-esterify the pectin so that a gel can form. Apples themselves contain natural but variable amounts of PME and until recent years this has been a very considerable constraint on the process. In the last decade or so, however, specialist PME preparations, which also have other applications in fruit processing, have appeared on the market. These enzymes are not readily obtainable in small quantities, but for cidermakers in the UK and Europe a suitable PME plus calcium chloride is now available as a French kit sold under the name 'Klercidre', and a small scale keeving kit is also available in North America (an up-to-date list of keeving suppliers is given on my website).

A kit is undoubtedly the easiest way to get started with keeving, although the calcium chloride is relatively easy to purchase on its own. If you are trying to source the enzyme yourself, it is very important to stress that these PME enzymes are not at all the same as the commonly available pectic enzymes used for clarifying purposes. These PME preparations are very specialist and in fact must not contain any trace of the other polygalacturonase or 'depolymerizing' activities which are used for juice clarification. The pectin must only be de-esterified; if it is de-polymerized too, then the gel will never form.

It is also important to stress that the PME and calcium chloride must never be added together but only as two separate sequential operations. Some people recommend adding the PME first and then the calcium chloride solution a few hours later. The PME dosage level cannot be given here since it depends on enzyme strength which varies by manufacturer. Enzymes may be provided either in stabilized solution or in solid form (adsorbed onto a carrier). PME is relatively stable and if stored in a fridge may lose about 10 per cent of its activity over a year.

Availability of calcium chloride and PME enzymes has helped to take keeving from the realms of art closer to that of a science (and if you cannot get hold of the commercial enzyme then even the addition of calcium chloride is a considerable help) but it is still not a 'recipe book' operation. One important step is the 'maceration' of the pulp, that is, leaving it for twenty-four hours prior to pressing. A major purpose of this is to solubilize as much pectin as possible – it is important to have enough pectin to form a good gel, and by leaving the pulp overnight it has the chance to solubilize and leach out of the cell walls. There is some evidence that it is useful to add some of the PME enzyme at this stage too, but pectic enzymes are also inhibited by the pulp tannin so it is best to reserve some for addition to the juice also in the normal way.

Juice blends

In traditional keeving the PME did not work well in acidic (low pH) fruit and hence bitter-sweets were the fruit of choice; bittersharps like Kingston Black would not generally keeve. This was obviously something of a drawback since it left the fermentation poorly protected against microbial infection at such a high pH. Fortunately, conventional wisdom has now been turned on its head with the new enzymes which are active at much lower pH so it is now realistic to perform successful keeves on blended juices including bittersharps down to pH 3.6 and even below. This is a considerable advance and allows keeving to be much more widely practised for well-balanced juice blends, which was frankly tricky before.

Wild yeast fermentation

It will be noted that a wild yeast fermentation is required and that just a little sulphite is used (in the traditional scheme, the barrels were pre-sulphured). Cultured yeasts obviously cannot be used here since they are

A *chapeau brun* with fermentation about to break through; racking is needed.

far too vigorous; indeed it is interesting that the French industry is still very keen on slow mixed microflora successional yeast fermentations. On the other hand, incipient fermentation is required to start within a few days since the cap must be buoyed up by trapped gas bubbles. In the absence of the traditional pre-sulphured barrels, I prefer to add sulphite to the original juice at around one-quarter of the recommended level for the pH (see earlier) to control unwanted organisms, so that sufficient wild yeast growth occurs to raise the cap in a reasonable time (about a week). It sometimes happens that some mould growth takes place on top of the cap before it is fully risen and ready to rack. In this case, the mould can be carefully removed to prevent it spreading, but since the clear juice will be racked from underneath the cap there should be little danger of it contaminating the juice itself.

Racking and bottling

Racking the clear juice from between the *chapeau* and the sediment can be something of a challenge, but is made easier by translucent HDPE tanks with bottom taps and a small pump. In traditional designs for French cider factories the keeving tanks were set up above ground level, so that the keeved juice could be gently drawn off by gravity from below the *chapeau*. This operation should not be rushed and the potentially fragile cap should not be allowed to break up. The cap can vary in firmness and crustiness quite considerably and not all the keeved juice will be easily recovered. Sometimes it is possible to let the cap re-form and take a second crop of juice after a couple of days. But some irretrievable volume loss, maybe up to 20 per cent, must be expected during keeving. It is also critical to watch the process daily and to rack off just before the cap begins to break up and to fall back into the vat. If you are a hobby cidermaker

A second-crop consolidated keeve in a translucent tank, ready for racking.

and this point is reached on a Tuesday, it may be too late if you wait until you have more time at the weekend. By then, all may be lost!

Once the fermentation is under way, it needs monitoring and then some sequential racking to slow it right down with a view to bottling at say SG 1.015 or 1.010. Recent French work has demonstrated that the optimum time for the first racking, for best removal of nutrients, should be once the SG has dropped by 10 degrees from its initial starting point. Later racking will also be required once the target SG is reached, to ensure that it has stabilized.

Traditionally, a keeve might be set up in

November and the bottling carried out in April. It will then take several months to develop 'condition' in bottle. You must be sure that the fermentation is imperceptibly slow by then (a maximum loss of 1–2 degrees SG over three weeks) and champagne bottles are recommended in case of accidents, because in theory you may be over the limit at which the bottles could burst should all the sugar re-ferment. In France, keeved ciders are bottled in champagne bottles with slightly undersize special *cidre bouché* corks (25×38mm) and stored upright. Then, if excess gas should develop, it can escape slowly past the cork rather than blow the bottle. The bottles should be stored in a cool place (seventeenth century writers refer to them being stored in cool running spring water to avoid them becoming 'potgun' cider).

If you are taking your keeving seriously, you may want to invest in a good quality narrow range hydrometer to get the most accurate SG measurements and you should also take account of the appropriate temperature correction when you make those measurements (if not at the calibration temperature which is normally 20°C). The apparent SG rises by about two points as the temperature drops from 20°C to 10°C and such a temperature change can easily obscure any changes due to slow continued fermentation. Precise SG measurement is not necessary for most normal cidermaking, but it is important when keeving.

Keeving is not a fully controllable process, certainly not for the beginner, and your first attempt may not be a success. There are many factors to balance for a successful keeved cider and it is not a turnkey operation, nor is it for those who are easily discouraged. Balancing the required factors relies on judgement and experience which you can build up over several seasons, to give you greater confidence and control. This was once part of the skill of the traditional cidermaker, although he knew absolutely nothing of the biochemistry behind it as we do now, and those skills largely became lost in the English-speaking world over the last century. But in the last few years a number of hobbyists and small commercial cidermakers outside France have re-developed the skills for themselves. In the twenty-first century, information is much more readily available, and I would advise anyone embarking on the process for the first time to read as much as you can around the subject from online articles and discussion groups. Anyone wanting a handbook to modern cider making by keeving in the French style should also read *Guide pratique de la fabrication du cidre*, published in 2006 by l'Institut Français des Productions Cidricoles (http://www.ifpc.eu/kiosque.html).

5 WHEN THINGS GO WRONG

So far we have looked at cider making when everything goes according to plan. Inevitably, however, there will be occasions when things do not work out as expected, so this chapter deals with various problems and some possibilities for putting them right.

MY CIDER HAS A PROBLEM

Slimy pulp

If you are lucky enough to have genuine cider apples to use and they are not stored for too long, you are unlikely to have problems with slimy pulp. Apart from its other qualities (bittersweet, bittersharp, and so on) true cider fruit has also been selected over many generations to press cleanly and to leave a dry and handleable pomace. Remember, though, that the pulp should not be milled up too small, even with genuine cider apples – we are not aiming for apple-sauce. The ideal size for pressing is little nuggets of apple each about the size of a small pea, which gives the best compromise between juice yield and ease of pressing.

With dessert apples, however, no matter how carefully you mill the fruit, there is always a tendency for pectin to leach out of the cells and to be partially broken down by the natural fruit enzymes while pressing. This is particularly true if the fruit has been stored for any length of time. The result of this is a 'cheese' of slimy pulp, which clogs up the press-cloths, oozes through

them, and makes it impossible to get a decent yield of juice. Under these circumstances you may find that light continued pressure for some time gives you a better result than a quick hard squeeze. Even so you may have to resort to other measures. In the US, 'press-aids' such as wood pulp or rice hulls are sometimes used, mixed with the apple pulp to provide better drainage pathways. An alternative is to press mixed loads of fruit if you can, the better with the poorer. If you can press a mixture of desserts and bittersweet, the tannin and the superior structure of the bittersweets will help to offset the poor characteristics of the dessert fruit.

The best solution is to apply a pectic enzyme to the pulp. In this case, you are aiming to complete the total breakdown of the pectin, to overcome its partial breakdown in the apple which is causing all the problem. You can use the same type of pectolytic enzyme which is used in the juice to eliminate hazes as described in Chapter 3, although the dosage rate will need to be about twice as high.

The enzyme should be well-mixed with the pulp and allowed to stand, at 55°C for two hours or at room temperature for up to twenty-four hours. For most people, holding warmed pulp is not an option, and an overnight incubation in the cold will be the most practical solution. Next day, the pulp should press much more cleanly and easily, and you will not then need to add any more enzyme to the juice before you start to ferment. This technique is suitable for 'conventional' cider making – it cannot of course be used if you are trying keeving because the pectin will

Sloppy pulp oozing through cloth.

be broken down too far and it will be impossible to obtain the required calcium gel.

Stuck fermentation

A fermentation is said to be 'stuck' if it stops working while there is still fermentable sugar left. In traditional craft cider making, as described, many fermentations are intended to stick, precisely so the cider can be bottled with some degree of residual sweetness. But if you want to ferment to dryness and the cider is not obliging, you must look to factors such as nutrients (amino nitrogen and vitamins) and temperature.

It is usually worth adding nutrients, aerating the cider by vigorous stirring and splashing for thirty minutes or so to encourage yeast growth, and raising the temperature to 15°C or 20°C. A recommended nutrient addition in this case is a fixed dose of thiamine (0.2 ppm) plus a variable dose of 50 ppm ammonium sulphate or phosphate for each 10 points of SG yet to be

fermented. If this does not work you may need to re-pitch with a good vigorous yeast starter, perhaps one that is tolerant of existing alcohol such as a champagne yeast. These measures nearly always do the trick. Of course it is important to check that the cider really is stuck first, by taking a proper SG measurement. I have heard of cases where people believed their cider to

Vitamin B1 and yeast nutrient (ammonium phosphate) for sticking fermentations.

be stuck because they could not see bubbles passing through the airlock due to slight leakage around the cork, yet they had not measured the SG to check – in fact the cider had already finished fermenting!

MICROBIOLOGICAL PROBLEMS DURING FERMENTATION AND STORAGE

In a good and active fermentation, properly sulphited and protected by an airlock, few problems should arise. In slower fermentations or during storage, there are a number of classical microbiological problems which may crop up.

Film yeasts

Film yeasts (generally of the genera *Candida*, *Pichia* or *Hansenula*) will commonly contaminate a slow and unsulphited fermentation if not under airlock, or a poorly sealed cider in store. The organisms are present on the fruit and thrive in aerobic conditions, so they typically appear on the top of ciders where they will start to break down the sugar or the alcohol. Their presence is often detected by a strong smell of esters, somewhere between vinegar and the solvents used in nail-varnish remover. In small amounts these compounds are important contributors to the overall flavour of cider but as soon as they become obvious then you have a potential problem. Sometimes more unpleasant musty or oxidized flavours are formed instead. The yeasts themselves form a light grey greasy/powdery film on the surface of the cider, breaking up into small white sheets and dropping to the bottom of the vessel when disturbed. If the

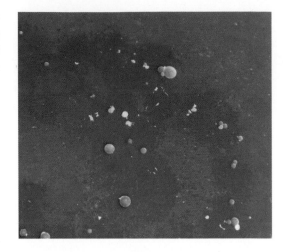

A light dusting of film yeast showing characteristic trapped bubbles.

film is gently pushed to one side with a finger, it will 'ruck up' in a characteristic way.

Prevention is better than cure but, if film yeasts take a hold, keep the vessel well topped-up to exclude air and maybe add 50–100 ppm SO_2 to keep the organisms in check. Generally they only

A heavy growth of film yeast, which has been pushed gently to show how it rucks up.

occur as a thin film on the surface where access to air is easiest. Film yeasts are more common in ciders than in grape wines because of the lower alcohol level. A light growth of film yeast is a warning sign that action is needed. The cider may still be quite usable if infection has not gone too far but extra care must be taken during handling to make the conditions for their growth as unfavourable as possible. Vessels where infection has occurred should of course be properly sterilized before re-use.

Acetobacter

Acetic acid bacteria (vinegar bacteria) of the *Acetobacter* family are sometimes confused with film yeast because they too tend to grow on the surface of poorly stored ciders. They oxidize the alcohol to acetic acid directly and so the cider smells and tastes of vinegar rather than of solvent. *Acetobacter* at high levels and at temperatures above 20°C tend to form brown jelly-like sheets on the top of the cider but, unlike film yeast, these do not break up when shaken but fall to the bottom all in one piece.

They are aerobic organisms just like the film yeasts, however, so the same preventative and remedial measures should be effective. If the cider is too acetified (vinegary) for your taste, it can sometimes be partly neutralized by the careful addition of potassium carbonate although this will reduce the total acid as well. Alternatively the cider can be stored in a tightly sealed container until next season, when it can be blended back in with fresh pomace at the rate of 50 litres per 50kg and re-pressed and re-fermented with a fresh yeast inoculum which may consume some of the acetic acid. It is also possible to re-ferment an affected cider simply by adding a little extra sugar (no more than 10 grams per litre) and a fresh cultured yeast. The same techniques may be worth trying for

ciders badly affected by film yeast. However, by the time a cider becomes seriously and visually affected by *Acetobacter*, it may be best to take it straight on to vinegar anyway.

Proper sulphiting at the outset of fermentation and during storage, coupled with rigorous exclusion of air, should prevent this problem occurring. *Acetobacter* are often spread from place to place by fruit flies.

It is worth pointing out that a cider which simply smells vinegary may well be unpleasant but is not necessarily anywhere near actually being vinegar. A small amount of ethyl acetate plus a touch of acetic acid (0.14 per cent is the maximum allowed in the NACM Code of Practice) is enough to be reminiscent of vinegar and even to be described as acetic, but in true vinegar all the alcohol (say 5 per cent) is converted to an equal amount of acetic acid. The specific production of cider vinegar is covered in the final chapter.

Other forms of acetification

Farmhouse ciders

It has to be said that many so-called 'farmhouse' ciders can be quite badly acetified, particularly the poorly-made 'scrumpies' which are still sold to unsuspecting tourists in the West Country. There is probably some truth in the assertion that older generations of cider-drinkers became conditioned to these flavours since they were an integral part of the rough ciders which were then on offer and where sulphur candles were not in use to 'sweeten' the barrels and the cider was not well stored. The same was probably true of many wines until the widespread adoption of glass bottles and cork closures in the eighteenth century. Nowadays, however, most of us would regard acetified flavours as undesirable and it is certainly quite possible to make a fine and well-flavoured 'traditional' cider without them.

Lactic acid bacteria

There are a number of organisms which can cause an acetified flavour – not only the film yeasts and acetic acid bacteria but also some species of lactic acid bacteria. In some styles of cider, such as in Asturias (Spain) the acetic note is regarded as a desirable part of the flavour profile. In this case it is believed to come from the presence of lactic acid bacteria which act at the same time as the yeast in the relatively warm weather prevailing in that region at harvest time.

Cider sickness

Cider 'sickness' is a disorder caused by bacteria of the genus *Zymomonas* (other types of which are utilized in the tropics for the production of palm wine). These organisms ferment sugars in the same way as yeasts, but they also produce large amounts of acetaldehyde and other flavour components which are said to give an odour of lemon or banana skins. In France, this disorder is known as *framboisé,* since the odour is regarded as raspberry-like. The acetaldehyde also combines with the cider tannin to give a milky haze and the cider quickly becomes insipid and 'thin' in body.

This problem only affects sweet ciders or those with residual sugar which are also low in acid (pH higher than 3.8), and is manifested by a renewed and turbulent fermentation. Ciders which are naturally sweet and low in acid (such as French traditional) are obviously under greatest threat from this organism. Unfortunately it is totally resistant to SO_2 so there is no easy control. The normal recommendation if ciders begin to become sick is to raise the acidity to 0.5 per cent and to add an active fermenting yeast complete with nutrient. You will lose your 'sick' sweet cider but with a bit of luck you may end up with a much healthier dry one which will be some recompense.

If the sick cider is already in active bacterial fermentation you will just have to let it take its course and then fine it and blend it off when all the sugar has gone. Once again, all equipment which has been in contact with cider 'sickness' should be well sterilized before re-use. Sick cider is rarely if ever encountered in the UK today since few ciders fulfil the criteria for infection, but may become more frequent if keeved sweet and low acid ciders become more common.

Oxidized 'sherry-like' aromas

Ciders that taste or smell flat or sherry-like have also been affected by air, but unlike acetification this normally happens without the intervention of microbes such as yeast or bacteria. It is a chemical reaction which follows from the oxidation of polyphenols (tannins) by air to generate small quantities of hydrogen peroxide. The peroxide further oxidizes some of the fermentation alcohols to aldehydes and it is these aldehydes which give the characteristic sherry-like aroma. This can only happen in the absence of free SO_2 which binds to the aldehydes and is one of many reasons why commercial ciders are always protected by SO_2 in store, in addition to the rigorous exclusion of air. If small amounts of aldehydes should be formed, they are scavenged by the SO_2.

Once a cider has become noticeably sherry-like it is difficult to reverse, although the addition of 50 ppm SO_2 may be tried. Re-fermentation as described for acetified ciders may also help. But prevention is so much better than cure. It is not for nothing that an old French cider-making aphorism has it that *L'air est l'ennemi mortel du cidre* (air is the mortal enemy of cider).

Sulphury smells

If your cider smells of rotten eggs, drains or is generally 'unclean' then it may have a sulphur taint. Unfortunately most volatile sulphur compounds in fermented beverages are odour-active at very low levels, even parts per trillion in some cases, so these can be very noticeable even when present in minute amounts.

Many ciders do smell slightly sulphurous when in the course of active fermentation but this usually disappears quickly at the end of fermentation. If the smell does not disappear, excess hydrogen sulphide (H_2S) or a related compound may be the cause. This can be tested by taking a small sample of the offending cider in a glass and dropping a brightened copper penny or a piece of copper wire into the sample. After ten minutes or so, its aroma should be assessed against an untreated control glass.

If the offending aroma has disappeared or is reduced, it is possible to treat the bulk cider by the addition of copper (cupric) sulphate. This is a permitted practice for winemaking in the EU but only very small amounts of copper are used. (Excess copper can have adverse effects on both cider colour and flavour by encouraging unwanted oxidation as described later.) The addition required is one part per million which is an extremely small amount to measure. The best way to do this is by 'serial dilution'. For instance a 1 per cent solution can be made up by dissolving 5g of copper sulphate (a flat level plastic teaspoon) in 500ml of water. Then 5ml of this solution (a level plastic teaspoon) can be dispensed into 50 litres of cider to give the required level. Wait a day to see how well it has worked; one (or exceptionally two) further teaspoons may be added if required. The copper combines with the hydrogen sulphide to form cupric sulphide which is insoluble. It is also possible to buy bentonite impregnated with copper salts (such as Kupzit) which does the same job but minimizes the amount of residual copper passing into the cider.

The chemistry of sulphur in wines and cider is exceedingly complex, and if disulphide compounds have been formed after some time in storage it may be necessary to 'reduce' them before copper treatment by the prior use of ascorbic acid (Vitamin C). A professional winemaking textbook should be consulted for further details. It has been claimed that sulphur taints were not so much of a problem in a previous era when brass or bronze (copper alloy) fittings were common on tanks and pipework, since the transient contact with the metal acted to remove them. Some people nowadays even suggest running cider through a short length of copper piping for this reason!

The ultimate cause of such flavours is generally yeast related and is connected with the metabolic pathways for sulphur-containing amino acids. In some cases nitrogenous nutrients added before fermentation, especially with some cultured yeasts, will prevent the problem. Because there tend to be two peaks of H_2S production during fermentation, some authorities recommend 'split' additions of nutrients with half being added before fermentation and the remainder after about one-third of the sugar has been consumed.

Mousiness

Mousiness is unmistakable and deeply unpleasant to those who can recognize it, although individual sensitivity varies widely from person to person. The flavour is best likened to the smell of a mouse-cage, although some people think it is closer to bread or freshly-baked biscuits or crackers. Oddly enough the chemicals responsible for these flavours (acetyl pyrrolines and tetrahydropyridines) are all the same. They exist in cider in a combined (salt) form and are only slowly liberated when the cider is tasted, depending on the pH of the taster's mouth. Since this varies from one individual to another, different people respond differently and in any case the flavour takes several seconds to develop as the free compound is liberated.

You cannot smell mousiness, only taste it, unless you make the cider alkaline to liberate it into the headspace – you can do this by adding a pinch of sodium bicarbonate to a small glass of the cider and then sniffing it. This defect arises from the metabolism of the amino acid lysine by unwanted species of lactic acid bacteria or by the spoilage yeast *Brettanomyces*. It also requires some oxygen for its formation. Preventative measures therefore include the correct use of sulphur dioxide at all times, and cider storage in the absence of air.

Unfortunately there are no ways of removing mousiness once formed. The cider cannot be blended off, because of its strong taint potential even at high dilution. It must be thrown away and all vessels which contained the cider must be sterilized to eliminate the contaminating micro-organisms.

An old picture of a viscous ropy cider being poured.

bacteria during yoghurt-making and which provide its texture.

Ropiness does not generally occur where SO_2 has been used. It can be ameliorated if the cider

A dextran gel found in the bottom of a vat after MLF.

OTHER STORAGE PROBLEMS

Ropiness

Ropiness or oiliness is a curious condition which occurs sometimes in low acid ciders in bottle or in store. When the cider is poured it assumes the consistency of a light oil or of a slimy ropy texture like raw egg white, although the flavour is not much affected. This is due to the slow growth of certain forms of lactic-acid bacteria which produce polysaccharide (dextran) gels. These are similar to those formed by related

is transferred to an open vessel, well stirred to break the gel and treated with 100 ppm of SO_2. Fining with bentonite and gelatin (see later) may also help to bring down the bacteria and the gel. Sometimes you will find this gel when cleaning out a cider barrel which has undergone a natural malo-lactic ferment.

Blackening and greening

Discolouration of ciders (apart from the normal and desirable golden-orange colour of partly oxidized tannin) is nearly always caused by metals. Iron gives rise to blackening and copper gives greener hues, due to oxidation reactions between the metal, the tannin in the cider and the oxygen in the air.

Often the colour does not develop until a bottle is opened and the air can get in as the drink is poured – the colour then develops in minutes or hours. To confirm this, a freshly-opened bottle should be poured into two glasses. To one glass is immediately added a good pinch of citric acid, while the other glass is left untreated. If the treated glass darkens at a significantly slower rate than the untreated glass, then iron is the probable cause since the iron is 'chelated' and made less active by the citric acid.

There is not much that can be done to cure the problem although re-bottling in the presence of citric acid may be considered. An old fashioned remedy, which may still be of value, is the addition of fresh wheat bran to the cider at the rate of 75g per 50 litres of cider. The bran needs to be well mixed in, settled and then the cider racked or filtered off. The 'phytic acid' (a complex natural phosphate) in the bran traps the metals and removes them. A technique known as 'blue fining' can be used on a commercial scale to remove metal ion contamination but only in the hands of a trained chemist.

Such problems will never arise if the proper sort of processing equipment is used so that free iron and copper cannot get into the cider. The generally accepted upper limits for their presence in cider are 5 ppm of iron and 1 ppm copper (the NACM Code of Practice allows 7 and 2 ppm respectively). As described earlier, trace amounts of copper can actually remove sulphur taints.

Hazes and deposits

Many people making a traditional product will be quite happy with a certain amount of residual haze in their cider and will not expect it to be 'gin clear'. The cider will generally 'drop bright' after fermentation if bittersweet cider apples have been used, or if dessert apple pulp has been pre-treated with pectolytic enzyme. One of the properties of a good modern wine yeast is its ability to flocculate well and to form compact 'bottoms' after fermentation. Yeast cells are large enough that, other things being equal, they should settle to the bottom of a vat over a few weeks. If using a 'wild' yeast, things may be more unpredictable in this regard due to surface charges on the cell walls and so forth. Sometimes a cider starts sparklingly bright, but then annoyingly develops a haze or sediment later. There are a number of possible reasons for this.

Microbial hazes

Microbial hazes are caused by various spoilage yeasts or by heavy infestations of bacteria. Most of these have been covered previously although there is one slow-growing yeast (*Saccharomycodes ludwigii*) which forms clumps at the bottom of the bottle in sweetened ciders without affecting flavour very much. Generally, microbial problems should be avoided by proper attention to cleanliness and hygiene.

The only reliable way to tell whether a haze is microbial in origin is to look at it under a high-powered professional microscope (500× magnification). This is hardly practicable for the domestic cidermaker unless you have a friend or colleague with access to a suitable laboratory. If you do, ask them to look for yeasts (about 10 microns in size) or for bacteria (about 0.5 microns in size but often in pairs or in chains). 'Phase contrast' illumination is best if available – otherwise the slides must be stained to render the microbes visible.

Pectin hazes

Pectin hazes were described in an earlier section. Sometimes they show as a uniform cloudiness and sometimes as easily disturbed clots or strings floating in the bottle. If you want to be sure of preventing them, you must use a pectolytic enzyme which is added at the beginning of fermentation. If you think you have a pectin haze in the finished cider, add one part of cider to two or three parts of methylated spirit (denatured alcohol) in a small glass and shake well. The pectin will form a gel or a clot, or possibly strings if there is not much pectin there. If pectin is confirmed you can try adding some pectolytic enzyme to break it down although it will not be so effective in the presence of alcohol. Otherwise you must just live with it and remember to do better next time.

Tannin hazes

Tannin hazes are sometimes the most frustrating, because they may develop in store in ciders which may have been bottled completely clear. They occur particularly in ciders made with bittersweet fruit where the tannin levels are relatively high. Over time these tannins can polymerize together to generate large molecules which eventually become so big that they drop out of solution. Sometimes they form a haze, while sometimes they coalesce to a compact sediment. Often they cause a 'chill-haze', where the product becomes cloudy when put in a refrigerator for summer drinking but was quite stable at room temperature, or they may appear during winter storage if the cider was bottled before a snap of cold weather (a repeated warming and cooling cycle is a good test to indicate potential tannin haze).

The tannins are also responsible for much of the 'bite' of traditional bittersweet ciders so it seems a pity to remove them. Sometimes, however, bittersweet ciders may be so bitter or astringent that it is worth lowering the tannin levels for reasons of taste, as well as for haze stability. The 'fining' procedure described later can be used for either. It can also be used for gross clarification before sheet filtration or racking, or perhaps to remove 'ropiness' or 'sickness' bacteria. Do remember, though, that fining a low tannin cider will make it even more insipid.

FILTRATION

Although large commercial cidermakers nearly always filter their product, a craft cidermaker may want to think twice before investing in filtration equipment. How sparklingly clear do you really need your cider to be? There are plenty of good modern sheet (depth) filters available, of different degrees of fineness, such that the coarse sheets will remove gross particles and the fine sheets even offer so-called sterile filtration (that is, they potentially remove all yeasts and most bacteria). But some sorts of hazes, for example pectin and other polysaccharides, are not well removed by filters and often just blind them and reduce throughput rather quickly.

All sheet filters will absorb considerable amounts of flavour and colour from a cider

A small frame filter unit (right) and pump (left); filter sheets are inserted between the plastic separators prior to use.

until the sheets are saturated and equilibrium is reached, which may take several tens or hundreds of litres, depending on scale. Rather than discard these 'fore-runs', it may be possible to recycle them back into the feedstock so they are not lost. But the slight gain in cider clarity after all this work may simply not be worthwhile.

So the pros and cons of conventional filtration for craft cider making need to be carefully weighed. The use of 'cross-flow ultrafiltration' has become widespread in the mainstream industry over the last twenty years but the equipment is still too costly for most small scale users.

It is possible to combine sheet filters for clarification followed by cartridge membrane filtration if true sterile filtration and sterile bottling is the aim (*see* Chapter 3). However, to take full advantage of sterile filtration, the filter units and all downstream pipework and storage vessels

and bottling equipment must also be sterilized (with steam or specialist chemicals) and maintained in that state during use, which demands a level of complexity and microbiological control which is not generally within the scope of the amateur or the smaller producer. Sterile filtration is an unforgiving process and just one weak link in the chain may be enough to allow contamination by yeast or bacteria to take hold and to prejudice a complete batch of cider.

FINING

An alternative way of clarifying ciders is by the traditional use of 'fining'. There are many different ways of fining although the principles are the same for all. The tiny particles of beverage haze are electrically charged, which is why they do not coalesce, because 'like charges' repel each other and keep them in suspension. If we add a material with an opposite charge we can neutralize the charges so the particles will then clump together and settle out.

Add protein and bentonite

In ciders the tannin or other particles of debris tend to be negatively charged and so we add a positively charged material which is usually a protein. Traditionally, egg white or fresh slaughterhouse blood was used – one egg will treat about 10 gallons of cider. Nowadays special gelatins are used to provide the protein. If too much gelatin is added, the cider becomes 'overfined' and we get a persistent gelatin haze instead, so it is wise to add some bentonite at the same time. Bentonite is a negatively charged clay which mops up any spare gelatin.

Appropriate grades of gelatin and bentonite are available from specialist winemaking suppliers. Do not use domestic 'cooking' gelatin which has quite the wrong physical properties. Isinglass works well for beer but do not use it in cider because it has the wrong properties due to the difference in pH. With grape wines bentonite on its own is often used as fining to remove protein hazes, but ciders contain much less protein hence protein hazes do not form, so bentonite alone is of little value to the cidermaker.

Trials before bulk treatment

Ideally it is best to run tests to find out how much gelatin and bentonite are required in a particular situation. Also, because fining with gelatin will tend to remove some tannin from a cider (and is sometimes done deliberately for this purpose), small scale trials are essential

before treating a large bulk of cider. For instance a 1 per cent stock solution of gelatin should be made up in warm (not boiling) water, and a 10 per cent stock slurry of bentonite should be creamed up separately in warm water too. Then set up a series of six flasks each containing 200ml of cider and an appropriate amount of bentonite as shown in the left hand columns of the table. The appropriate volumes of gelatin solution are then added from a pipette or a small syringe as shown and the flasks are well shaken. After leaving for several hours, the flask which gives the greatest amount of clarification with the least amount of ingredients, should be chosen for scale-up according to the right hand columns of the table.

Full scale fining

For full scale fining the bentonite should be creamed up in a small quantity of cider and then well distributed in the bulk. The appropriate amount of gelatin should be made up as a 5 per cent solution in warm water and added to the bentonite-treated cider in a thin stream with constant stirring before being allowed to settle for several days. If the main purpose of the exercise is to reduce tannin levels, rather than to clarify the cider, the gelatin solution should be added first, allowed to stand for two hours after stirring and then followed by the bentonite. Ideally the cider should be kept as cool as possible after the addition of fining agents, to encourage the most efficient sedimentation.

After fining, a deposit will be thrown and a clear cider should remain above it. This can then be racked off, filtered and bottled accordingly. The handling involved during fining will obviously cause some aeration which should be kept to a minimum for all the reasons previously discussed. The addition of 50 ppm SO_2 at this stage will also be helpful to prevent oxidation.

Cider Fining with Bentonite and Gelatin			
Test (per 200ml cider)		Full Scale (per 100L of cider)	
Bentonite (ml of 10 per cent suspension)	Gelatin (ml of 1 per cent solution)	Bentonite (grams)	Gelatin (grams)
1	1	50	5
1	2	50	10
2	2	100	10
2	4	100	20
4	4	200	20
4	8	200	40

There will also be some irretrievable loss of cider volume in the 'bottoms' (the sludge which settles after fining).

Modern substitutions

Kieselsol

A more efficient substitute for bentonite, is a colloidal silica or silicic acid often known by the German term *kieselsol*, which forms much more compact bottoms and much more quickly than bentonite. If the kieselsol is supplied as a 30 per cent solution, it should be diluted to a stock solution 1:10 with water and used in place of the bentonite in the test fining above. For full-scale fining, the kieselol should be used undiluted at the same rate given as for bentonite. Kieselsol has been around for over fifty years but until recently was not widely available for amateur use, whereas it now seems to be readily available from the specialist winemaking suppliers.

Chitosan

Another modern fining agent, which may be used on its own or in combination fining as a gelatin substitute since it is positively charged, is called 'chitosan' and is prepared from crab shell and other crustacean waste in the US and the Far East. The 'chitin' (a polymer of N-acetyl glucosamine) which forms the animals' exo-skeletons is treated to de-acetylate and solubilize it and this yields 'chitosan'. It has several specialist medical applications especially in the field of wound dressings. As a fining agent, chitosan is becoming more widely available from the specialist beverage suppliers and works well in ciders. Dosage rates for individual preparations should be obtained from the suppliers.

Combination kits

In recent years home winemaking shops have started to offer 'two-part' finings which comprise both gelatin (or chitosan) and kieselsol, in separate packages. The amounts are pre-measured, for example for 20 gallons of wine, and are simply dispersed in sequence into the cider or wine following the directions given. Because this is a two-part fining, the risk of over-fining is much diminished and test fining is not generally required. For amateur use this system is highly recommended. However, bear in mind

Two-part kieselsol and chitosan finings as sold to home winemakers.

that no finings may effectively remove pectin or other polysaccharide-based hazes.

Over the last twenty years fining for clarification of commercial ciders has rapidly become almost obsolete since the advent of cross-flow ultrafiltration, as this offers a means of removing suspended solids continuously to a high degree of clarity without blockage. The synthetic ultrafilter membranes rarely have to be replaced in normal use and are cleaned by backflushing and chemical washing. However, this is a costly technique and likely to be of value only in a factory situation, not for smaller scale craft use.

6 APPLE JUICE, CIDER VINEGAR AND PERRY

The majority of this book has dealt with the making of cider. This final chapter looks instead at how we can stop the process one stage earlier to make apple juice and how we can take it one stage further to turn our cider into vinegar. I have also included a few remarks about perry.

APPLE JUICE

Apple juice is in some ways more difficult to make than cider and indeed it can scarcely be regarded as a traditional product at all. Until the recognition by Pasteur in the mid-nineteenth century that fermentation was caused by yeast converting sugar into alcohol, the difference between juice and cider was somewhat obscure and of little practical importance in any case. It was known that fresh juice was an unstable commodity and that it would soon start 'working' – that is, fermenting – so that cider was the only practicable end-product. Not until the invention and understanding of pasteurization (thermal sterilization) was there any practical way of preserving the juice with its full content of sugar. That is the fundamental process of juice-making – to preserve the sugar from the fruit without it turning into alcohol – and this can really only be done by heat treatment to kill the yeasts, or by deep-freezing or chemical additions to stop them growing. All these processes require a relatively sophisticated technology, by traditional standards.

The fruit

The milling and pressing requirements for juice making are no different from cider making, since both begin at the same point. The fruit requirements, however, are rather different. In cider we need high sugar to turn into alcohol, some acid to benefit the course of fermentation and for flavour balance, and some tannin to give body to the final blend. In juice the most important feature is the 'Brix/acid' ratio, which is the percentage sugar divided by the percentage acid. The preference for this ratio is very much determined by where you live. In the UK and the rest of northern Europe, a ratio of 15–20 would be considered appropriate. In the US, ratios as high as 30 are acceptable, but to a British palate the juices would be considered very sweet.

Up to a point the absolute values of sugar and acid do not matter so much as the ratio. Thus, a juice with 10 per cent sugar and 0.5 per cent acid would be judged equally as acceptable as a juice with 15 per cent sugar and 0.75 per cent acid, both having a ratio of 20. From this it is easy to see that a Bramley juice with 10 per cent sugar and 1 per cent acid gives an unacceptably low ratio of 10, while a sweet cider cultivar with sugar of 15 per cent and acid of 0.2 per cent would have an unacceptably high ratio of 75. A bittersweet cider cultivar, with high tannin levels too, would also be quite inappropriate for juice making, since it would have too dry a mouthfeel and not enough acid. You can get away with most bittersharps for juice, though, and some, such as Browns Apple, have acquired quite a reputation recently as good juice apples too, because the tannin levels are not very high.

In practice good juices can be made from a variety of dessert apples and those which have interesting flavours in their own right (for example Cox, Egremont Russet or Ashmead's Kernel) generally make the most interesting juices too. Early apples which are delicate in flavour, such as Worcester Pearmain, may make rather characterless juices, though Discovery does tend to make a crisp and fruity juice which captures the early fruit character. 'Single variety' juices have now become quite popular at UK farmers' markets and other specialist outlets and offer a surprisingly wide range of flavours.

Sweet apples can always be blended with Bramley to improve their acidity, while Bramley itself can always have some sugar added to improve its B/A ratio even though it will never make a first-class juice. A good general starting point is three parts dessert apple to one part Bramley. Although the fruit must be clean and wholesome it can be small or misshapen. Indeed most commercial apple juice is made from such fruit, which is cosmetically unsaleable on the retail market. But the fruit must be well-washed and none of it must be mouldy. If you would not be prepared to eat it as fresh fruit, then it is not fit for juice-making!

THE CASE OF PATULIN

Patulin is a mycotoxin produced by various fungi (notably *Penicillium expansum*) which are found in rotting fruit. When first discovered in the 1940s, as a spin-off from wartime penicillin research, it was actually tested as an antiviral treatment against the common cold and was the subject of one of the very first modern controlled medical trials. However, it did not work in that role, and it was not until the 1970s that it was also found to be present in apple juice which had been made from poor quality fruit. It is mutagenic in certain laboratory tests, which means that it may have the potential to cause cancer in animals although this has never been satisfactorily demonstrated. Nonetheless, good practice requires that its presence should be kept to a minimum, and its level in regular apple juice for sale in the EU is now legally controlled to 50 ppb (parts per billion) or below 25 ppb in baby food.

Patulin will scarcely be present in apples which are hand graded to eliminate all rots before juicing. However, one fully rotten apple in a couple of hundred good ones can be sufficient to contaminate the juice to the 50 ppb level, so care must be taken that the grading and washing are efficient.

Graded fruit that is juiced immediately after picking, or is 'barn stored' and re-graded before processing, is unlikely to give any patulin problems. Some commercial juice manufacturers, working with controlled atmosphere fruit taken from store late in the season (that is, in the spring and summer following harvest), have found problems with patulin production even though the fruit looks sound. Research has shown that this is mostly associated with bruised or damaged fruit, especially if it has been allowed to stand at room temperature for several days after coming out of controlled atmosphere cold store, rather than being juiced immediately. The changes in temperature and oxygen exposure seem to stimulate the fungi to germinate, even though the hyphae cannot be seen with the naked eye and they are not yet sporulating (there is no visible sign of mould). For most craft producers, juicing only in high season, this is not a problem. (Incidentally, patulin does not survive alcoholic fermentation as it is converted to another less toxic component called escladiol.)

Large apple juice producers test every batch for the presence of patulin. Unfortunately this cannot be done except in a specialist laboratory and tests are expensive to have done by contract analysts. If you are selling the juice, depending on the scale of your operation, 'due diligence' may demand that you have testing done on occasional batches through the season. For fuller information, UK producers should contact the Food Standards Agency for up to date advice.

CLOUDY OPALESCENT JUICE

One of the best juices to make, in the opinion of most connoisseurs, is the pale cloudy opalescent juice which has become very popular in the UK in recent years. Curiously, although the basic process was developed in the US and Canada in the 1940s, it is scarcely used on that continent at all at present, where cloudy but brown 'fresh apple cider' is a much more popular alternative.

Known as the Pedersen process after its inventor, it was introduced to the UK by the Long Ashton Research Station during the 1970s and quickly became adopted by producers of high quality juice. The fruit is chosen, washed, sorted, milled and quickly pressed in the normal way. After screening through a coarse mesh, Vitamin C (ascorbic acid) is added directly to the juice at the rate of 500 parts per million (5g per 10 litres of juice). Pure powdered ascorbic acid should be used for this – it will be much cheaper and more convenient as a winemaking sundry than as a formulated vitamin from the chemist shop. The ascorbic acid allows certain biochemical reactions to happen in the juice which develop and maintain its fresh and varietal flavour, but it prevents the oxidation and browning of the tannins which make it look unsightly and lead to sedimentation.

Opalescent apple juice.

Freezing

Now the juice must be preserved without delay. If you have room in your freezer it can be poured into plastic containers, or into polythene bags packed into cardboard shells. Once frozen, the juice can be withdrawn from the cardboard and stored as frozen polythene bricks. Do not ever put glass bottles in the freezer, since they will crack as the juice freezes and expands. The juice can be thawed for use as required, but it will not keep long after thawing because the enzymes and yeasts that were present in the juice originally will still be active. Nor will the cloud be 'set' and it may settle out rapidly when thawed. However, freezing is very convenient if you have the space to cope with it.

Pasteurization

The alternative is pasteurization. For this, the juice must be run into good quality glass bottles (not plastic) which can be sterile sealed by heating. Crown capped beer bottles, available from home brewing suppliers, will do quite well, as will good quality screw-capped bottles sealed with new 28mm screw caps (the bottles, though not the caps, are re-usable).

The bottles are filled to within a couple of inches of the top, to allow for foaming and thermal expansion, and placed in a large pan of cold water which is put on the stove and rapidly heated. A false bottom in the pan will prevent the bottles 'bumping'. I have found that a stainless steel catering pan with a perforated steel false bottom makes a useful sterilizing bath for stove top use. The bottles should be as far immersed in the water as possible. Using a digital kitchen thermometer, place the thermometer in the centre bottle of the group and continue heating until the temperature of the juice itself reaches at least 74°C. At this temperature all the yeasts should be destroyed.

Take the hot bottles out of the pan with sturdy rubber gloves and cap them immediately. Do not stand the hot bottles on a cold metal surface or the cold shock may crack them. Whether using crown-cap or screw-cap bottles, seal them tightly and then lay them on their sides to cool slowly, so that the hot juice can sterilize the inside of the cap. Do not hurry the cooling process.

The bottles may then be stored at room temperature indefinitely until required, although the juice itself always tastes best if chilled for a few hours before drinking, and the quality is probably best if drunk within a year or two. The presence of the ascorbic acid goes a long way towards eliminating any 'cooked' flavour. If processing a second batch, do not put cold bottles of juice into the water bath at 70°C or more since the shock may crack them. Bring the water

Pasteurizing juice on a stove-top waterbath. Note the use of the digital thermometer.

bath down to around 50°C with additional cold water first.

Heat treatment of this sort is highly satisfactory although the very occasional broken bottle may result during pasteurization.

Mould growth very rarely occurs in the bottles during storage; this is much more likely after the bottles are opened and the air can get in to germinate the mould, because some mould spores can be extremely heat resistant, although yeasts are quite easily killed. For this reason the bottles, once opened, should be stored in the refrigerator.

An advantage of heat treatment is that it actually 'sets' and stabilizes most of the desirable apple juice cloud, which does not happen when the juices are frozen. People often imagine the opalescence is apple cell material, when in reality it is a protein/ pectin cloud.

The observant reader may notice that the pasteurization conditions for apple juice are far more stringent than they are for sweetened cider (see Chapter 4), and may wonder why. In fact, the target conditions for a cloudy apple juice are in the order of 500 PU or so, compared to only 50 PU for a fermented cider. The main reason is that the alcohol in the cider provides an extra constraint on renewed yeast growth and so less heating is required to inactivate the already stressed yeast. In addition, the presence of solids in opalescent juice means that the yeasts are physically more protected from the effect of heat than they are in cider.

It is also possible to pasteurize apple juice packed as 'bag-in-box', in the same way as it is for ciders. However, since the temperature required for juice is higher than that required for cider the bags are on the very limit of what their laminate material will tolerate. Although I have pasteurized 'bag in box' juice successfully as an amateur, I might be wary of recommending it for commercial use. Also once the bag is opened for use, the chance of re-contamination

from airborne yeasts via the tap could be significant. A fermenting and exploding box of juice would be very messy! However, I understand some small commercial producers are doing this successfully.

On a large scale, purpose-built pasteurizers may be purchased, or a handyman can convert a stainless steel sink with an immersion heater and a false bottom to maintain the correct temperature. Small electrically heated pasteurizers which hold a dozen bottles or so are also available for hobby use. Bulk pasteurization of the juice itself in a tank or a saucepan is a poor alternative to in-bottle pasteurization, because of the danger of overheating and excessive oxidation at 'hot spots'. It is also very difficult to hot-fill the bottles aseptically on a small scale. In large commercial operations flow-through heat exchangers are used and the hot juice is filled straight into clean warm bottles under 'aseptic filling' conditions. On the biggest scale, HTST treatment and Tetra-Pak cartons are used.

If you like something a little different, you can try adding 15 per cent of tinned mango purée

Small electric waterbath pasteurizers each holding twelve bottles.

to a batch of juice before bottling and pasteurization. The juice will foam a bit more during pasteurization and may make it a bit tricky to read the temperature correctly, but the result is well worth it.

Heat *vs* chemical preservation

I do not recommend chemical preservation with sorbate or benzoate as an alternative to heat treatment of juice. There will be a large number of wild yeast cells present in a fresh pressed juice and at moderate levels (200 ppm) these preservatives cannot be guaranteed to protect a juice against fermentation for more than a few days. In any case preservatives are not permitted in the EU in apple juice for retail sale. Larger amounts of benzoate (up to 1000 ppm), which are permitted in the USA, will be more effective for longer periods of time but there may also be adverse flavour issues. Eventually some yeast and moulds will overcome even these high levels of benzoate.

A particular benefit of heat treatment is that it kills any contaminating pathogenic organisms harmful to human health such as *E. coli* or *Salmonella*. Until recent years it was thought that these organisms could not multiply at the low pH found in apple juice, but a number of unfortunate and fatal outbreaks of infection due to *E. coli* 0157H in North America have shown that this strain at least can proliferate in unpasteurized apple juice even when refrigerated. Although its origin is associated with animal manures, which should be nowhere near the apples in any case, there is always the chance of contamination by the droppings of wild animals such as birds and deer, which pasteurization will readily control.

In the UK and Europe unpasteurized farmgate apple juice has never been an article of commerce so this is not an issue, but it has long been popular in North America and is sold in the fall as 'fresh apple cider'. The US FDA (Food and Drug Administration) has therefore set a 5 log pathogen reduction standard for such juices, that is, the microbial load must be brought down by 100,000 times. This can be achieved by heat or by a special 'flow through' UV sterilization procedure. An advantage of the UV treatment, although it does not save on energy costs, is that it maintains a fresher and less 'cooked' flavour compared to pasteurization. However, it kills only the pathogens and does not inactivate the spoilage yeasts. Hence the juice will still ferment even if UV treated, though large amounts of benzoate will inhibit the fermentation for some time.

CLEAR JUICE

To make a clear golden juice it is necessary to destroy the pectin cloud and to allow a certain amount of oxidation to take place for colour development.

The most reliable way of doing this is to press out the juice as normal into a clean container, without the addition of any ascorbic acid. Add a pectolytic enzyme and keep the juice cool overnight to prevent yeast growth and fermentation. Next morning the juice should be golden in colour and should have dropped bright, leaving a sediment at the bottom. If not it may have to be fined with gelatin/bentonite (*see* Chapter 5) and left cool (but not refrigerated) for a further day.

Rack or strain the juice carefully into clean containers for preservation by freezing or by heat treatment as described in the previous section. Sometimes the colour becomes rather dark by this method and a small amount of ascorbic acid (100–250 ppm) may therefore be added before enzyming to inhibit oxidation. In some cases the addition of pectic enzyme may be unnecessary since there may be sufficient enzyme and calcium present naturally in the juice for it to 'drop bright' by itself overnight in the cold – but you will not know this until you try it.

Juices of this style tend to be less 'varietal' and have a more cooked character than those of the opalescent kind.

Warning: Explosion

Juices must never be bottled in a sealed container (especially in glass) without effective pasteurization.

If all the juice sugar ferments inside a closed bottle, it can theoretically develop an internal pressure in excess of 400 psi. This is more than enough to cause serious damage or injury when the bottle eventually explodes (as it almost certainly will). Just for comparison, even a properly designed champagne bottle is only expected to hold a pressure of about 100 psi.

CIDER VINEGAR

From a biochemical viewpoint, cider vinegar is the next step after cider itself on the road which converts sugar through to alcohol, thence to acetic acid and finally to carbon dioxide and water.

At each step the organisms involved gain energy from their environment – this, after all, is why they do what they do, and their metabolism is very little different from our own in most respects. Animals do not stop at the alcohol or acetic acid stage, but some micro-organisms do, and we can take advantage of this to provide the products that we want. Vinegar is simply a dilute solution (about 5 per cent) of acetic acid which results from oxidation of the corresponding quantity of alcohol by the aerobic bacterium *Acetobacter xylinum*.

To make cider vinegar we need to start with a fully fermented dry cider with a minimum 5 per cent alcohol content. Preferably, sulphur dioxide should not have been added because this may inhibit the conversion to acetic acid.

Contrary to all good cider making practice, we then need to leave the cider in a vessel with plenty of access to air and to ensure that *acetobacter* can get in, or alternatively the bacteria may be added in the form of a 'vinegar mother'. These organisms, fatal to good cider, are just what we need for vinegar.

The Orleans process

The traditional set-up for vinegar-making is known as the Orleans or barrel process and consists of a barrel laid on its side, three-quarters full of wine or cider with open access to air. The bung hole is lightly plugged or covered with gauze so that oxygen can get in but flies cannot. A 'vinegar mother' floats on the top of the wine and converts to vinegar at the rate of roughly 1 per cent per week so that a cider with an alcohol of 6 per cent will give a vinegar of 6 per cent acetic acid in a couple of months or so. The barrel must be kept warm, 20°C or above. Two-thirds of the barrel is then drawn off as vinegar, fresh cider is added and the cycle is repeated.

Modern vinegar factories do not use this method because it is far too slow. They use big fermenters (generators or acetators) with forced aeration and a very high population of acetic acid bacteria, which can convert a wine or cider to vinegar in just a few days or even hours. Efficient as the big fermenters may be, the advantage of the barrel process is that it has no moving parts and virtually nothing to go wrong. You just have to wait a good deal longer!

Setting up the system from scratch is the hardest part. Traditionally, a vinegar barrel was always started by adding an inoculum of old vinegar from somewhere else. In general though it will be no good for you to buy a regular bottle of vinegar from a store and hope to use it as a starter, since most modern commercial vinegars are both filtered and pasteurized and the *acetobacter* do not survive. However, there are a very few vinegars on the market which do claim to contain viable 'vinegar mother' and it might be worth hunting these down. If you wait long enough, though, wild acetic acid bacteria will almost certainly find their way in.

One plan is to keep an open jar of cider, covered with a coarse mesh, in a warm dark but airy place for as many weeks as it takes for a 'mother of vinegar' to form. Fruit flies (*Drosophila* species) may be an advantage here since they are likely to carry *acetobacter* about with them. It is wise to add about 25 per cent of commercial cider or wine vinegar to the jar to inhibit other non-acetifying organisms. Make sure that any vinegar you add does not contain any SO_2 or other preservative – this will be stated on the label.

Another method for generating a vinegar starter is to make a heap of fresh apple pomace, keeping it moist and preferably warm for several weeks. During this time it will ferment its residual sugars and natural *acetobacter* should then proliferate. Once it smells quite vinegary, the pomace can be squeezed out through a muslin bag and the resultant liquor (rich in *acetobacter*) can be used as a starter which will eventually develop a 'mother'.

It is also now possible to buy a starter culture of vinegar bacteria from at least one European winemaking supplier, which should soon form a 'mother' if allowed to develop in the appropriate conditions.

The 'mother' is simply a floating jelly-like raft of cellulose which is made by the *acetobacter* themselves to keep them close to the surface, since air is essential for their existence. Once you are sure you have a genuine gelatinous 'mother' and not

a powdery film yeast, and you can really smell the vinegar, you can pitch it into your barrel with the required amount of still dry cider and your Orleans process will be under way. Keep it warm, up to 30°C if you can, for best results.

Do not, whatever you do, use the same equipment and vessels for vinegar making as for cider. The risk of cross-infection is just too great and it is not worth spoiling your good cider by trying to economize in this way. Keep both operations entirely separate! If you are making vinegar close to your cider, as you probably will be, it is doubly important that your cider-making kit be properly cleaned and sterilized anyway.

Is it ready?

To know whether the vinegar is ready or not you really need to measure the acid. You can use a winemaker's acid titration kit for this but you must dilute the vinegar exactly ten times with distilled, deionized or rain water before you carry out the titration. Then multiply the result by ten. If the results from the kit are expressed as tartaric acid you must multiply them again by 0.8 to express the result as acetic acid. The minimum amount of acetic acid required by EU food law for sale as vinegar is 5 per cent.

Once the vinegar is made it can simply be run into bottles for use. On a domestic scale there is no need for pasteurization.

Cider vinegar from the Orleans process is generally fairly clear but it may develop a further haze on storage in bottle. This can be due partly to renewed growth of bacteria and partly to polymerization of tannin. You can fine the vinegar with gelatin/bentonite if necessary to reduce an existing or a potential haze. The 'two part' chitosan/kieselsol finings also work well. If it is then important to prevent further clouding, SO_2 at 50 ppm (that is, 2 Campden tablets per 10 litres) may be added just before bottling and this will inhibit both types of spoilage process.

Vinegar vats occasionally become infected with vinegar 'eels'. These are small and transparent nematode worms a few millimetres long, which live on the acetifying bacteria and which wriggle ceaselessly at the top of the vat. Although quite harmless they are generally unsightly and people do not like them. They may be destroyed by heating the vinegar to about 50°C, followed by fining or filtration after cooling. Or you can just leave them as a talking point for your guests – they will liven up any salad dressing!

PERRY

The fruit

Perry is the name given to a cider made from pears. Although, with the right additions and ameliorations any pear juice or concentrate may be used to produce a perry, the finest are generally held to be those made from true 'perry pears'. The best perry can indeed rival a light white wine, both in quality and (almost) in alcohol content.

Traditionally, these perry pears grew in a very limited area of the Three Counties of Gloucestershire, Herefordshire and Worcestershire, where huge perry pear trees many hundreds of years old may still be seen. They also grow in the cider areas of northwestern France, where *poiré* is also a traditional beverage, and in some parts of Switzerland and Austria. When grown on pear rootstock, rather than the dwarfing quince which is more common for dessert varieties, they are much larger than any apple tree and take a long while to come into bearing. 'Plant pears for your heirs' was a common expression.

There are many sorts of perry pears, as there are of cider apples, though they do not fall into the same classifications. Some are very tannic and low in acid, though, and need to be blended with the more acid sorts. All are pretty much inedible and many are so hard that they need storing for several months before pressing.

Perry making lends itself to experimentation for those who are so inclined, especially as regards the choice of raw material. A few small cidermakers in the south of England, but well outside the traditional Three Counties area, make perry from un-named wildling pear trees which produce hard and almost inedible fruit but a fine drink. Ornamental pears with similar fruit (such as the cultivar 'Beech Hill') have also been investigated and seem to blend well with dessert pears. These, like all perry and dessert pears, are seedlings or cultivars of the European pear *Pyrus communis* which is widely grown worldwide. However, some cultivars of Asian or 'Nashi' pear (*Pyrus pyrifolia*) are also being used to make light perries in the Pacific north-west of the US.

Different from cider making

Most perry pears have little pectin compared to apples, while some contain so much tannin that they can almost fill a vat with what they throw down while ageing. This tannin, once referred to as 'leucoanthocyanidin' but now more correctly known as 'proanthocyanidin' is much more polymeric than the sort found in apples and tends to be purely astringent with very little bitterness. Pears contain few airspaces between the fruit cells and so they do not float in water, unlike apples. Perry pears contain much more sugar than apples, hence more alcohol is developed in the drink. They also contain significant amounts of the unfermentable sugar alcohol known as sorbitol, which provides a greater natural residual sweetness than typically found in cider, and can also have a noticeable laxative effect at the concentrations found in perry.

A major acid in many varieties of pears is citric, rather than the malic of apples. Unfortunately citric acid, unlike malic, is also subject to breakdown into acetic acid and ethyl acetate by lactic acid bacteria, usually during storage. This is one reason why traditional perries tend to 'go acetic' much more readily than ciders. Careful use of sulphur dioxide during storage will help to prevent this.

Sources of information

Although craft perry making follows the same broad principles as for cider, it is a more skilful and generally less well understood operation, and there are few guiding textbooks to demonstrate the differences. For instance, more sulphur dioxide is needed prior to fermentation than for cider, since the pear naturally contains high levels of acetaldehyde which bind up the added sulphite. The best source of information on perry making is the out of print book *Perry Pears* edited by Luckwill and Pollard at the Long Ashton Research Station in 1963. This is available in facsimile and also in part on the Marcher Apple Network *Vintage Fruit* CD, which also includes a very useful article on the 'Principles and Practice of Perry Making' by Pollard and Beech. No further detail will be given here since this is such a specialist topic.

CONVERSIONS AND CALCULATIONS

APPROXIMATE TEMPERATURE CONVERSIONS

0° C = 32° F
4° C = 40° F
10° C = 50° F
15° C = 60° F
20° C = 68° F
25° C = 77° F
30° C = 86° F

LIQUID MEASURES

1 imperial gallon = 4.5 litres (L)
1 L = 0.21 imperial gallons

1 US gallon = 3.8 litres (L)
1 L = 0.26 US gallons

6 US gallons = 5 imperial gallons
1 hectolitre (hL) = 100 L

1 US fluid ounce = 29.6ml
1 US pint = 16 US fluid ounces = 473ml

1 imperial fluid ounce = 28.4ml
1 imperial pint = 20 imperial fluid ounces = 568ml

DRY MEASURES

1 kg = 2.2.lb
1 (avoirdupois) oz = 28g
1 teaspoon (US) is defined as 5ml for food labelling purposes.
1 teaspoon (UK) is conventionally 6ml.
1 metric teaspoon is 5 ml.

For many dry materials and powders, the 'bulk density' is around 1 so that a 'level teaspoon' gives around 5 grams by weight. However this is only an approximation and not valid in all cases.

SMALL QUANTITIES

1 part per million (ppm) = 1mg/litre
1000 ppm = 1g/litre = 0.1%
10,000 ppm = 10g/litre = 1%

SERIAL DILUTION

The technique of serial dilution can be used to obtain small doses with reasonable accuracy. For instance, a 1 per cent solution can be obtained by dissolving 5g of a solid (a flat teaspoon) in 500ml of water. Taking 5ml (a teaspoon) of that 1 per cent solution and diluting it in 50 litres of cider gives a dilution factor of 1:10,000. When multiplied by the 1:100 original dilution (1 per cent), this gives an overall final dilution of 1:1,000,000 or 1 ppm.

RESOURCES

WHERE TO GET EQUIPMENT AND SUPPLIES

In the UK and Europe

Vigo Ltd, Dunkeswell, Honiton, Devon, EX14 4LF supplies the professional and larger-scale market. Tel: 01404 892100. www.vigoltd.com.

Vigo Presses Ltd, Unit 4, Flightway, Dunkeswell, Honiton, Devon, EX14 4RD supplies the amateur and smaller scale market. Tel: 01404 890093. www.vigopresses.co.uk.

Both **Vigo** companies now trade separately but together they are the premier source of supply for wine and cider making equipment in the UK, and can generally supply to the EU too. The company's founder is a prize-winning cider maker himself.

Brouwland, Korspelsesteenweg 86, 3581 Beverlo, Belgium. Tel: +32 (0)11 40.14.08. www.brouwland.com. A Belgian based firm with a very wide range of winemaking equipment and supplies. The Brouwland website (available in several languages) lists local agents in many other countries. They also supply directly by post or courier into the UK.

The Home Brew Shop, Unit 3, Hawley Lane Business Park, 108 Hawley Lane, Farnborough, GU14 8JE. Tel: 01252 338045. www.the-home-brew-shop.co.uk.

The Home Brew Centre, 10 High Street, Keynsham, Bristol, BS31 1DQ. Tel: 0117 986 8568. www.homebrewcentre.co.uk. Both the Home Brew Shop and Home Brew Centre are good for mail order supply of sundries and chemicals in small quantities.

Hardwood Crafts, Peter Eveleigh in Bradford on Avon produces bespoke hand-made working apple mills and presses from English hardwood. www.hardwoodcrafts.co.uk.

SFM Technology, 9 Bancombe Court, Martock, Somerset, TA12 6HB. Tel: 01935 822285 www.fruitharvesting.com. SFM manufacture and sell apple harvesting machinery and fruit washers.

The **Vares Fruit Shark Mill** is now supplied by Vigo Presses (see above).

Bellingham and Stanley. Supply budget refractometers for purchase online on both sides of the Atlantic at www.refractometershop.com

Jigsaw Bag in Box Ltd, Unit 13, Suprema Estate, Edington, Somerset, TA7 9LF. Tel: 01278 722136. www.baginboxonline.co.uk. Jigsaw supply bag in box packaging in small quantities for craft cider producers.

In the US

Goodnature Products Inc., 3860 California Rd, Orchard Park, NY 14127. Tel: 716 855 3325. Toll free 800.875.3381 (within the US only). www.goodnature.com. Sells larger items of equipment (mills, presses etc).

Happy Valley Ranch, 16577 W. 327 Street, Dept. 8D, Paola, KS 66071. Tel: 913 849 3103. www.happyvalleyranch.com.

Correll Cider Presses, P.O. Box 400, Elmira, Oregon 97437. Tel: 541 935 3500. www.apple-journal.com/correll. Suppliers of smaller scale presses.

Oesco Inc., P.O. Box 540, Route 116, Conway, MA 01341. Tel: 1 800 634 5557. www.oesco-inc.com. Suppliers of larger scale equipment including bladder presses.

MoreFlavor, 995 Detroit Ave Suite G. Concord, CA 94518. Tel: 1 800 600 0033. http://morewinemaking.com.

Northern Brewer, 2221 Highway 36 West. Roseville, MN 55113. Tel: 1 800 681 2739. http://www.northernbrewer.com

Midwest Supplies, 2221 Highway 36 W. Roseville, MN 55113. Tel: 1 888 449 2739. http://www.midwestsupplies.com. MoreFlavor, Northern Brewer and Midwest Supplies are good for equipment, sundries and supplies.

WHERE TO GET CIDER APPLE TREES

In the UK

Thornhayes Nursery, St Andrews Wood, Dulford, Cullompton, Devon, EX15 2DF. Tel: 01884 266746. www.thornhayes-nursery.co.uk.

National Fruit Collection, Brogdale Farm, Brogdale Road, Faversham, Kent, ME13 8XZ. Tel: 01795 531888. www.brogdaleonline.co.uk. Will graft any tree in the Brogdale collection.

John Worle Ltd (Herefordshire), Tel: 07769 801394. www.johnworle.co.uk. John was previously orcharding manager for a large cidermaker and has many years experience.

Frank P. Matthews Ltd, Berrington Court, Tenbury Wells, Worcs, WR15 8TH. Tel: 01584 810214. www.frankpmatthews.com.

Keepers Nursery, Gallants Court, East Farleigh, Maidstone, Kent, ME15 0LE. Tel: 01622 726465. www.fruittree.co.uk.

Adam's Apples, Egremont Barn, Payhembury, Honiton, Devon EX14 3JA. Tel: 01404 841166. www.talatonplants.co.uk.

Bernwode Plants, Kingswood Lane, Ludgershall, Bucks, HP18 9RB. Tel: 01844 237415. www.bernwodeplants.co.uk.

Cider Apple Trees, 'Kerian', Corkscrew Lane, Woolston, Somerset, BA22 7BP. Tel: 01963 441101. www.ciderappletrees.co.uk.

Note: Cider fruit in the UK in season is rarely available on the open market but may sometimes be obtainable by personal enquiry from small growers or from orchards which are no longer being harvested. The Cider Workshop discussion group (see 'Internet Resources') can be a useful starting point for this.

In the US

Cummins Nursery, 1408 Trumansburg Rd, Ithaca, NY 14850. Tel: 607 592 2801. www.cumminsnursery.com.

Trees of Antiquity, 20 Wellsona Road, Paso Robles, CA 93446. Tel: 805 467 9909. www.treesofantiquity.com.

Raintree Nursery, 391 Butts Road, Morton, Washington 98356. Tel: 1 800 391 8892. www. raintreenursery.com.

Vintage Virginia Apples, 2550 Rural Ridge Lane, P.O. Box 210, North Garden, VA 22959. Tel: 434 297 2326. www.vintagevirginiaapples. com.

Big Horse Creek Farm, 1610 Old Apple Road, Lansing, NC 28643. Tel: 336 384 1134. www. bighorsecreekfarm.com.

Copenhaven Farms, 12990 Copenhoyer Road, Gaston, OR 97119. Tel: 503 985 7161. www.copenhavenfarms.com.

Willamette Nurseries, 25571 South Barlow Road, Canby, OR 97013. Tel: 503 263 6405. www.willamettenurseries.com.

Note: In North America, fresh (dessert) apple juice may often be obtained in season from local mills and presses. If you want to ferment it, though, be sure what you buy is preservative free. A very few growers, such as Poverty Lane Orchards, Lebanon, NH, may sometimes sell true cider fruit to small scale cidermakers.

Australia

Heritage Fruit Trees, 297 Back Raglan Rd, PO Box 35, Beaufort, Victoria 3373. www.heritage fruittrees.com.au.

Mia Apple Farm, 80 Joyce Lane, Mia Mia, Victoria. Tel: (03) 9701 3066. www.miapple.com. au.

Woodbridge Fruit Trees, PO Box 95, Woodbridge, Tasmania 7162. Tel: 04 1898 1997. www.woodbridgefruittrees.com.au.

Telopea Mountain, Invermay Road, Monbulk, Victoria.Tel: 04 1866 5880. www.petethe permie.com.

Balhannah Nurseries, Hartmann Road, Charleston, South Australia. Tel: (08) 8389 4557. www.balhannahnurseries.com.au.

CONTRACT BOTTLING

In the UK

Pershore College (Worcestershire) operating as **Avonbank Juice and Cider**. www.warwick shire.ac.uk.

Branded Drinks Ltd, Coleford, Gloucs. www. brandeddrinks.co.uk.

FURTHER INFORMATION

Internet resources

www.cider.org.uk. My own website contains additional technical and background information about cider making for which there is no space in this book and a link to some mill and press construction details.

www.ciderworkshop.com. The Cider Workshop website holds a diversity of information on small scale cidermaking and links to the Cider Workshop discussion group http://groups. google.com/group/cider-workshop.

Cider Digest. The US-based email can be found via www.talisman.com/cider and is the premier technical discussion group for serious craft cidermakers both in North America and further afield.

The Marcher Apple Network. www.marcher-apple.net. Publishes and sells the *Vintage Fruit* CD referred to in Chapter 2.

Books

Hobby Books

The New Cider Maker's Handbook – A Comprehensive Guide for Craft Producers by Claude Jolicoeur (2013). Chelsea Green Publishing, Vermont, US. Claude is a serious hobby cidermaker and mechanical engineer from Québec. This book combines his personal perspectives with solidly researched information from other cidermakers worldwide, to create a detailed manual which is both practical and inspirational. With a North American focus and particularly strong on aspects such as press design and naturally sweet ciders.

Cider – Hard and Sweet by Ben Watson (2013). The Countryman Press, Woodstock, Vermont. The third edition of this book is an excellent historical and practical guide written by an American author from a US perspective but with a fair bit of European background too. Ben Watson is active in the Slow Food movement in the US northeast and a hobby cidermaker. Thoughtful and highly recommended.

Cider Enthusiasts' Manual by Bill Bradshaw (2014). Haynes Publishing, Yeovil, UK. A richly illustrated photo-book by a professional photographer and cider enthusiast, showing the steps involved in small scale cidermaking from apple to glass, complete with directions for constructing a mill and a press. Oriented to the UK

West Country using traditional cider fruit and processes from that area, and includes a section on pressing through straw!

Making Craft Cider – A Ciderist's Guide by Simon McKie (2011). Shire Publications, Oxford, UK. A book aimed at the small domestic producer written by a West Country hobbyist. Similar in its coverage to the *Real Cidermaking* book by Pooley and Lomax.

Real Cidermaking - On a Small Scale by Michael Pooley and John Lomax (1999). Special Interest Model Books, Poole, Dorset. Describes how to make cider on a small scale at home but in a simpler and more naturalistic style than from this book. Unfortunately the keeving section recommends the addition of ten times more calcium chloride than it should. This book also includes plans for a small scale cider press, in this case of the 'slatted basket' type.

Cider – Making, Using and Enjoying Sweet and Hard Cider by Annie Proulx and Lew Nichols (2003). Storey Publishing, Massachusetts, USA. This is the third edition of this long-standing practical American handbook. I liked the first edition (1980) rather better – it had more pictures and drawings (and a personal acknowledgement to me and all my Long Ashton colleagues, which got dropped due to a typo in the second edition and was not restored in the third!). Although detailed, it is beginning to look rather dated now. Contains plans for a press similar to the one I made for myself. Annie Proulx is the famous author but before she became famous!

Cider Apples – The New Pomona by Liz Copas (2013) is a private production available directly from the author herself from www.lizcopas.com and replaces and updates her previous *Somerset Pomona* though with less historical detail concerning cidermaking itself. Contains descriptors and photographs of around 150 UK cider apple varieties.

Ciderland by James Crowden (2008). Birlinn Ltd, Edinburgh. This is a lyrical and well-illustrated exploration of UK cider history and of some modern UK cidermakers.

Professional Books

Cider and Juice Apples: Growing and Processing, edited by R.R. Williams (1988); *Cider Apple Growers Guide* by Liz Copas and Roger Umpleby (2011). Both these books have limited availability but should be obtainable by mail order from the Hereford Cider Museum www.cider museum.co.uk.

'Cidermaking' in *Fermented Beverage Production* (2nd edn 2003) edited by A.G.H. Lea and JR Piggott, Kluwer Academic (Springer).

See also: 'Cidermaking' in *Oxford Handbook of Fermented Foods* (2014) edited by C.W. Bamforth and RE Ward (Oxford University Press).

Cider and Perry Associations

National Association of Cidermakers, The Bounds, Much Marcle, Ledbury, Herefordshire HR8 2NQ. Tel: 01531 660832. www.cideruk. com.

Farmhouse cider winners at the Bath and West Show.

Three Counties Cider and Perry Association, www.thethreecountiesciderandperry association.co.uk.

South West Cidermakers Association, www.sweca.org.uk.

Welsh Cider and Perry Association, www. welshcider.co.uk.

Training and competitions

Courses

Mitchell Food and Drink. Formal courses on cider making are offered in the UK and the US by Mitchell Food and Drink. www.mitchell-food-drink.co.uk.

Pershore College. www.warwickshire.ac.uk.

Competitions

The UK

The premier cider and perry competitions are held during spring and summer by the Bath and West Show at Shepton Mallet, the Three Counties Show at Malvern and the Cider Museum Hereford International Competition. A unique show is held in May at Putley, near Ledbury, where all the entrants comprise the judging panel. Many other local shows and cider festivals are held all over the country, often in conjunction with beer festivals.

The US

The Franklin County Cider Days in western Massachusetts are attended in November by many US and Canadian craft cidermakers keen to swap ideas and taste each other's products. www.ciderdays.org. The increasingly important Great Lakes cider competition is held annually in Michigan. www.greatlakescider.com.

Australia

In Australia the annual Cider Awards competition is organized by Cider Australia. www.cideraustralia.org.au.

INDEX